Economics and the Gospel

by

Richard K. Taylor

A primer on shalom
as economic justice

A Shalom Resource
Published for
Joint Educational Development

United Church Press
Philadelphia

This book is one of four adult primers on shalom, edited by Charles McCollough. Forthcoming primer titles are:

Waging Peace: A Way Out of War
Next Steps Toward Racial Justice
Shalom Is . . . Whole Community

Scripture quotations, unless otherwise indicated, are from the *Revised Standard Version of the Bible,* copyrighted 1946 and 1952 by the Division of Christian Education, National Council of Churches, and are used by permission.

Joint Educational Development—an ecumenical partnership for the development of educational systems and resources. Christian Church (Disciples of Christ), The Episcopal Church, Presbyterian Church in the United States, Reformed Church in America, United Church of Christ, and United Presbyterian Church in the U.S.A.

Library of Congress Cataloging in Publication Data

Taylor, Richard K
  Economics and the Gospel.

  (A Shalom resource)
  Includes bibliographies.
  1. Christianity and economics. 2. United States—Economic conditions—1961- I. Joint Educational Development. II. Title.
BR115.E3T38   261.8′32′50973   73-12570

Contents

Foreword

This book in the Shalom Curriculum tries to face head on a subject that is as complex and controversial as it is critical to the people who seek to live a moral life. It is critical because we live in a money economy where all essentials—food, clothing, shelter—require a constant and increasing flow of money income. The subject is as controversial as a 17th century theological war with all the accompanying saints, heretics, condemnations and actual warfare. People now fight and die for economic ideologies instead of religious doctrines.

Such a curriculum, inspired by the biblical vision of shalom, which seeks to overcome conflict, could not avoid dealing with this battlefield of economics. Richard Taylor was selected as its author because he is a participant in a new economic alternative that attempts to be free of economic bondage, a bondage that normally gives us only two options: a degrading, isolated life of poverty or a life locked into competitive scrambling for money to support one's life-style. Richard Taylor writes clearly about the complex subject of economics with a layperson's perspective of how to survive in our time free of either bondage. He speaks in a personal way with the authority of one who is doing it himself, and suggests ways others can become economically free.

His own manual for survival is the Bible. He goes to the Bible to see its simple truths and he rubs the words of the Bible up against the economic facts of our lives. The sparks that fly suggest visionary hopes for a more just arrangement of shared resources where cooperation rather than competition is not only the means of economic survival but also a new creative basis for service to others. He describes the specific life-style he and his family are living and relates his biblical and economic findings to national and global problems with suggestions about how we as individuals and groups can work at solving these problems.

5

Central to this book is the affirmation that economics is not subject to inevitable historical conditions or "invisible hands." Rather God's "hands" and justice rule economics and all of history. Economic problems are not mystical givens to which we all must adjust. They are not in a morally neutral realm where ethics is off limits. They are human problems that people, especially religious people, can understand, analyze and control for the good of all. This book is a simple, but powerful introduction to the economics of shalom.

C.McC.

Introduction

I can still see in my mind's eye the dark hallway we entered, with its falling wallpaper and grubby floor, the old men trying to keep warm around a wood stove in an otherwise heatless apartment in winter, the stinking hall toilets shared by many families, the mothers trying to cook family meals over hotplates, the desperate techniques used to keep rats from biting children, the cockroaches pouring down from a pipe over the children's bed.

I suppose in some ways this book began then, back in the late 1940's, when, along with other middle-class, suburban high school students, I was first introduced to the slums through a program called "weekend workcamps." We spent Saturdays and Sundays in low-income areas of the city, working with the residents to paint and plaster the ancient apartments they rented. And because we tried to work with, and not for, the people, I can remember getting to know them as we labored on the decaying walls, and finding that they were human beings like myself, who had done nothing to "deserve" their inhuman plight. The major difference between us was that they were poor and Black, while I was well off and white. This gave me a look at a world different from the tree-lined suburban streets where I grew up. It generated in me a desire for a society in which no one would have to suffer the degrading conditions I had witnessed.

I doubt whether these experiences would have had the same impact on me had they not seemed to contradict so drastically the Christian faith that I was learning at Sunday school. Were these not human beings made in the image of God? Why must they undergo such suffering? Why must they live in conditions not fit for animals, much less for children of God?

Other events occurred in my life that seemed to heighten the contradiction between these conditions, between the faith I learned and social and economic realities:

- Growing up in a Christian fellowship that taught religion, not as a separate compartment of existence, but as something to be practiced in daily life.

- Reading religious proclamations such as: "We must overcome poverty, disease, fear, injustice and prejudice" and "To work for these ends is part of true religion."[1]

- Hearing and having to answer monthly "queries" addressed to the group's membership that asked: "What are you doing, as individuals or as a [religious] meeting . . . to create a social and economic system which will so function as to sustain and enrich life for all?"[2]

- Hearing speakers at religious meetings describe the realities of slums and poverty, asking the listeners to measure the present social order against Christ's standard of a brotherly kingdom not based on selfishness

- Attending the weekend workcamps described above.

- Working with the American Friends Service Committee after college, in community development projects in Central America, where I saw the privilege and wealth of the elite against an overwhelming background of destitution, and noted the role of American corporations such as United Fruit and the ease with which the United States government supported oppressive dictatorships. Particularly, travelling in Guatemala after the United States-sponsored overthrow of the Left-leaning Arbenz regime and seeing firsthand the hollowness of "democracy" in the new United States-supported government of Castillo Armas.

- Working in the summer on a factory production line, experiencing its monotony and boredom and talking with a press operator who told me how he felt when an accident at a machine sheared off some of his fingers.

- Working with a Black community organization in a city slum area and learning about high unemployment, consumer fraud, and housing exploitation by landlords.

- Joining the national staff of Dr. Martin Luther King's Southern Christian Leadership Conference at the time of the Poor People's Campaign and being deeply impressed by Dr. King's growing conviction that America's problems were not just a matter of the destructive impact of racism on minority groups, but the destructive impact of economic structures on all poor people.

• Engaging in several years of study of our political and economic system, trying to better understand its strong and weak points, and searching for a vision of how our institutions could be less destructive and could do more to support human dignity.

• Visiting other countries[3] and studying and experimenting with means of nonviolent social change and a simple life-style that makes time available to pursue what one believes in.

• Discovering that most available jobs lock a person into a boring, thwarting use of energy, and discovering how difficult it is to have a normal life without a constant struggle to make more and more income, which leads to less and less vocational freedom.

• Discovering further that it is possible to break out of the job-debts-nine-to-five syndrome. By requiring less income to live (a family of four can live on $5,000 a year), it is possible to raise a family, enjoy a freer life, and do the kinds of things one affirms in faith.

This thought, study, and experience have brought me to certain views that I think are shared by many Christians, Jews, humanists, and others who have been moved to look hard at a world where people suffer so much.

I am convinced, for example, that poverty, hunger, slums, exploitation, and degrading human conditions should not be tolerated and can be changed. There is particularly no need for them in a wealthy nation such as the United States. I believe that the purpose of economic and political institutions should be to promote and enhance the dignity and well-being of each member of society and to achieve, so far as is humanly possible, the universal common good. I believe that Christians and Jews are called to pay attention to history and to work for a more just, human society that will be more in harmony with the coming shalom about which the Bible teaches. I have become more and more persuaded that the teachings of Jesus (for example, about not laying up treasure on earth, living simply, not grasping for money or possessions) are not only ethically sound but also requisites for survival in a world where overconsumption is leading to war and ecological destruction.

This is not a textbook on economics. Its purpose is not to explain institutions such as the stock market or phenomena such as the balance of payments. Its purpose is to try to look at economic life in the United States from a Judeo-Christian viewpoint, to ask how our economic order rates in the light of these teachings, to ask if it is possible to conceive of and work for economic arrangements more in accord with our Judeo-Christian values. It focuses on the United States, not because it is particularly good or evil, but because the writer and readers (most likely) are responsible for what happens here and are able to act within its borders.

I will try to be fair in the chapters ahead, but I am not striving for a "balanced" outlook in the sense of a neutral review of the main currents of Christian economic thought. This book was not conceived to be "value free." What I want to convey is one viewpoint to stimulate thought, discussion, and dialogue. I hope that this text will be useful for group study, for individual reflection, and for action.

CHAPTER 1

A Theology of Economic Justice

SECTION I: BIBLICAL GUIDELINES

From a religious point of view, what do we mean by "economic justice"? This is a difficult question, because for 200 years we have rarely looked at the economic system from a theological point of view or from a viewpoint of the ethical good of the whole. When economics and theology are discussed together, it is usually on the level of individual ethics.

This is so in part because in 1776 the philosopher and economist Adam Smith propounded an idea that was to become one of the most influential of Western culture: If each individual, investor, business firm would simply pursue its own self-interest, its own best financial advantage, within the framework of a competitive society, an "invisible hand" would see to it that the good of the whole was achieved.[1] Given such a philosophy, individuals felt free to pour their energies into their own acquisitive economic pursuits, confident that their seemingly selfish behavior would in reality contribute to the welfare of society at large.

The doctrines of Adam Smith have not been followed rigidly and dogmatically in many areas of Western economic life. There has been the Keynesian revolution, which gives government a role at least equal to the invisible hand in guiding the economic system. But Smith's ideas and those of similar thinkers have provided, and still do provide, much of the ideological framework within which Americans and others look at economics.[2] A prominent economist and presidential advisor echoes this point of view even in the 1970's when he writes that "the social responsibility of business is to increase its profits."[3] The good of the whole community is either reflected in, or assumed to follow from, profitable business.

Can these ideas be harmonized in any way with the teachings of Christianity? Can we imagine Jesus walking through Galilee, urging everyone to pursue his or her own selfish interests, to seek personal financial gain and not worry about the needs of others? Would it not be nearer to the spirit of Christ to say that everyone should lovingly pursue the well-being of each member of the human family, thus cooperating with God in assuring the common good? The only invisible hand in Christian teaching is the hand of God, and when we grasp it, we are led *away* from self-interest to love our neighbor as ourselves.

By contrast, the ideas of Adam Smith and others like him have led to what philosopher Richard Lichtman calls "the alienation of economic activity from moral concern."[4] Can Christians or Jews accept this separation of economic and moral concerns, either as individuals or as a part of society as a whole? After all, we stand in the tradition of Old Testament prophets who said, "Thus saith the Lord" to both kings and men of wealth, flinging some of their most powerful indictments against the *economic* injustices of their day. And we affirm a Creator whose concern and laws extend to the whole of life. However difficult it may be to find the answer, we are obligated by our faith to keep asking: What does God want us to do and to be in all aspects of our lives, economic and political as well as personal and social?

When we ask this question, we begin to overcome the alienation of economic activity from moral concern. We stop relying on an invisible economic hand to solve our problems. We begin to put together a normative framework, an overall perspective, within which economic activity and economic institutions can be judged. We begin to get glimpses of better ways of doing things, which seem more in line with our religious values. We begin to think through, in short, a *theology of economic justice*.

Let us look at some of the elements that might go into such a theology, focusing particularly on the biblical roots basic to Judeo-Christian thought. And, as we look at biblical insights, let us try to sense behind and through the words of scripture the concern and will of God for economic life. We are not seeking intellectual principles; we are seeking the guiding, empowering Spirit that led people in the past and that can guide and strengthen us today.

Protest Against Injustice

Historically, the world has been a place where great wealth and great destitution have existed side by side, and where some have gained power and privilege by oppressing others. In the Bible, we are "thrown into orations about widows and orphans, about the corruption of judges and affairs of the market."[5] We are confronted by language that, according to Abraham J. Heschel, expresses a "breathless impatience with injustice."[6] This leads to the first great biblical theme in relation to economic life, *a passionate protest against oppression, exploitation, and injustice.*

Whether we look at laws, prophetic teachings, psalms; or the gospel of Jesus, we find the constantly reiterated conviction that all oppression, including economic oppression, is contrary to the Divine will, provoking God to wrath and agony over his children's treatment of one another.

"What do you mean by crushing my people, by grinding the face of the poor?" asks the prophet Isaiah, speaking for God, to the leaders of Israel. (Isaiah 3:15) Punishment is in store, he says, for those "who keep writing oppression, to turn aside the needy from justice and to rob the poor of my people of their right." (Isaiah 10:1–2) The writer of Ecclesiastes laments that power is on the side of the oppressors, and tears are on the side of the oppressed, "and they had no one to comfort them." (Ecclesiastes 4:1) The Spirit of the Lord calls Jesus "to set at liberty those who are oppressed" (Luke 4:18) and he preaches woe to leaders who neglect "the weightier matters of the law, justice and mercy and faith." (Matthew 23:23) God's holy name is profaned, says the prophet Amos, when people "trample the head of the poor into the dust of the earth, and turn aside the way of the afflicted." (Amos 2:7)

Indeed, the call to end oppression and to establish justice is not just the philosophical thinking of creative minds, but the demand and promise of the Creator of heaven and earth. When humans heap up oppression and deceit, "they refuse to know me, says the Lord." (Jeremiah 9:6) "Justice is more than an idea or a norm. Justice is a divine concern."[7] The Lord himself loves justice. (Isaiah 61:8) He "executes justice for the fatherless and the widow." (Deuteronomy 10:18) He brings terrible doom to people and nations who do not act in righteousness. "Seek justice, correct oppression," (Isaiah 1:17) says his commandment. "You shall not oppress your neighbor," (Leviticus 19:13) says his law. The glory of human life is not in riches or might or wisdom, but in understanding and knowing God, "that I am the Lord who practice kindness, justice, and righteousness in the earth; for in these things I delight, says the Lord." (Jeremiah 9:23–24) "He who oppresses a poor man insults his Maker, but he who is kind to the needy honors him." (Proverbs 14:31) People fall away from such a high calling, but they can, with God's help, change. "So you, by the help of your God, return, hold fast to love and justice and wait continually for your God." (Hosea 12:6)

The God of Israel is thus seen and felt as a participant in human affairs, with a burning concern for good relations between people. Nations, as well as individuals, are to seek righteousness. Our problems befall us because we do not seek justice and love, and this separates us from God, the ground of our deepest well-being, our shalom. (Isaiah 59:2, 63:10)

Concern for the Needy

The Divine concern for justice does not reflect preoccupation with an abstract concept of equity. The Bible reflects God's involvement in human history, his concern with what happens on earth, and his urgent desire to save the victims of oppression. Thus the second great biblical theme to consider is God's love for humankind, a love expressed in *caring and concern for the whole human community, but especially for the poor, the weak, the defenseless.*

Justice is not important for its own sake; the validity of justice and the motivation for its exercise lie in the blessings it brings to man . . . An act of injustice is condemned, not because a law is broken, but because a person has been hurt.[8]

The "steadfast love of the Lord" is perceived as being so deep that human affliction grieves and afflicts God himself. (Isaiah 63:9–10) Those who suffer most excite God's compassion the most. "God's special concern is not for the mighty and successful, but for the lowly and the downtrodden, for the stranger and the poor, for the widow and the orphan."[9] Their misery is his.

If God so loves the needy, then it is up to those who seek him to express the same burning concern, the same caring. God finds guilty of great wrong those who have "surfeit of food, and prosperous ease, but did not aid the poor and needy." (Ezekiel 16:49) "If any one has the world's goods and sees his brother in need, yet closes his heart against him, how does God's love abide in him?" asks the writer of the First Letter of John. (1 John 3:17)

In the Torah, both prophets and formulators of law constantly stress God's command: "You shall open wide your hand to your brother, to the needy and to the poor, in the land." (Deuteronomy 15:11) Particularly emphasized is the responsibility to those who have no regular means of support, such as widows and orphans (Exodus 22:22; Deuteronomy 24:19, 26:12; Zechariah 7:10). But systematic practices exist to help all the poor, such as lending freely to the needy (Deuteronomy 15:7–10; Luke 6:35), leaving part of the harvest for the poor (Leviticus 19:9–10), and taking in a poor person and maintaining him (Leviticus 25:35). This was part of the law of the land in Israel.

Of course in the Gospels the theme of concern for the needy is seen as the mark of one who seeks to love God and neighbor and to inherit eternal life. (Luke 10:25–37) And in Matthew's story of the Last Judgment, the Divine identification with suffering humanity is expressed in "the King" waiting among the hungry, the thirsty, the stranger, the naked, the sick, and the imprisoned for people of compassion to respond to their need. (Matthew 25:31–46)

No one, says Rabbi Heschel, has the right to question "the principle that reverence for God is shown in reverence for man, that the fear we must feel lest we hurt or offend a human being must be as unconditional as our fear of God .•. . . To be arrogant toward man is to be blasphemous toward God."[10]

So much of this spirit is summed up in the words of the prophet Isaiah when he says:

> Is not this the fast that I choose:
>> to loose the bonds of wickedness,
>> to undo the thongs of the yoke,
> to let the oppressed go free,
>> and to break every yoke?
> Is it not to share your bread with the hungry,
>> and bring the homeless poor into your house . . . ?
> If you pour yourself out for the hungry
>> and satisfy the desire of the afflicted,
> then shall your light rise in the darkness
>> and your gloom be as the noonday.
> And the Lord will guide you continually.
>> —Isaiah 58:6–7, 10–11

Challenge to Hypocrisy

As concerned as the Bible is about people's relationships with one another, there is no attempt to substitute humanism for religion. God is to be worshipped and diligently sought, both for himself and as the power making righteousness possible. But outward observance of religion is an abomination without the practice of personal and social righteousness, and so another important biblical theme is *the critique of those who hypocritically carry on sanctimonious practices while practicing or ignoring economic (and other forms of) oppression.* The prophet Amos is convinced that Yahweh hates solemn assemblies, when those assembled have been trampling upon the poor, "but let justice roll down like waters, and righteousness like an ever-flowing stream." (Amos 5:11, 21, 24) Jesus warns his disciples against pious-seeming, well-to-do scribes, who make ostentatious prayers, but devour widows' houses. (Mark 12:38–40)

Value of Persons

Another biblical motif, which is integral to all that has been said so far, is *the preciousness, dignity, value, and potentiality of each individual member of the human family*. Humans are created in the image of God and are called to cooperate with him. When there is injustice and oppression in the land, it shows that "there is no regard for man." (Isaiah 33:8) "Human beings are so much more valuable than property," Jesus says, in effect, when healing a man with a withered hand. (Matthew 12:12) Individuals should be seen and treated as ends, not means.

Institutions to Serve Human Needs

If persons are given such great value in the scheme of things, then it is not surprising that *individuals and their institutions are called upon to serve human needs*. The sabbath was a crucial institution in the time of Jesus, but he angrily cut through its regulations and prohibitions to meet the need of a disfigured person. (Mark 3:1–6) When he said that the sabbath was made for man, not man for the sabbath, he established a criterion for judging all social (and economic) institutions: How do they affect human beings? Do they meet their needs?

In the Lord's Prayer, bread means more than loaves; it means all those basic things that we need to sustain us as God's children. It follows, then, that God gives bread only by the intermediaries of nature and human effort, and that the prayer for daily bread is a petition for a compassionate, God-sensitive human society that provides each day the basic needs of food, clothing, health, and shelter.

When the early Christians of the Book of Acts structured their common life, it was so that "there was not a needy person among them." (Acts 4:34) God's intention—not only for the church, but for society at large—was that the social order be a place where human needs are met and human personality brought to its full expression of love for God and neighbor.

Humanity as a Family

As biblical faith developed, *the analogy of humanity to a family* grew. Even with their conviction of their special relationship to God, the Hebrew writers sensed God's making of a people out of non-Jews: "Blessed be Egypt my people, and Assyria the work of my hands." (Isaiah 19:25) The family image was made concrete in Jesus' intimate sense of God's Fatherhood, expressed in his prayer to "Our Father" and in his reminder to his disciples that they are all brothers with one Father in heaven. (Matthew 23:8–9) God broods over humanity with the concern of human parents over their children—wanting each to experience fullness of life, working to encourage mutual concern, feeling agony if any is hurt or falls into misery.

In economics, may we not imagine God probing each economic system with a concern for its impact on his family of humans? "What does this economic order mean for my children? Does it lead some to exploit and oppress others? Does it condemn some to destitution? Does it encourage love or hate?"

Working for the Common Good

There is no expectation in the Bible that the weak and sick must labor, but *work is assumed to be a normal activity* for others. "Six days you shall labor and do all your work." (Deuteronomy 5:13) The apostle Paul is strict with idle busybodies who do not work, and he urges them to earn their own living, giving the stern command: "If any one will not work, let him not eat." (2 Thessalonians 3:10) However, he has a broad definition of work. Work is set in the context of building up the family and meeting human needs. The work that Paul urges upon the Thessalonians he calls "well-doing" (3:13), and when he speaks to the Ephesian church elders he describes his own toil as a means of helping the weak. (Acts 20:35) Thus work is seen as intentional, purposeful activity that contributes to the common good. Not just "a job," it is activity that takes some reality and transforms it for the good of the worker and others. People normally are active and busy at some kind of work, but is it constructive work?

Equality in the Human Family

Another biblical theme is that there should be *equality between members of the human family.* The early church father, Gregory of Nyssa, expresses the family context of equality when he says: "All things belong to God, who is our Father and the Father of all things. We are all of the same family; all of us are brothers. And among brothers it is best and most equal that all inherit equal portions."[11]

This was not a mathematical equality in which all have exactly the same possessions, but a sense of equity, a response to the Divine Father who judges "the world with righteousness and the peoples with equity" (Psalm 98:9) and whose will it is that none of his children be oppressed or destitute on the one hand nor puffed up with inordinate wealth and power on the other.

The biblical writers sensed that the economic order can easily slip into an unjust distribution of wealth, and they sought means to right the balance and to structure society so that there would be a more equitable sharing of wealth. The early Jewish "Jubilee Year," which was embodied in Israel's national law, called for the return of land that had been forfeited because of the owner's poverty (Leviticus 25:28) and the freeing of those who, because of poverty, had sold themselves as hired servants. (Leviticus 25:39–43) Although little is known of the actual practice of the return of property, the principle of a trustee relation to the land is evident.

When Paul writes of equality for the Corinthians, he is dealing with the church's responsibility to help impoverished Christians, but his words beautifully express the spirit of familial equality:

I do not mean that others should be eased and you burdened, but that as a matter of equality your abundance at the present time should supply their want, so that their abundance may supply your want, that there may be equality. (2 Corinthians 8:13–14)

The Danger of Wealth

Much of modern economics focuses on the accumulation of wealth, the need to raise the gross national product, and the expectation that the individual will pursue maximum financial gain. But running counter to this is the biblical theme *stressing the danger of riches and condemning the desire to accumulate wealth for oneself*. This is not particularly a theme of the Old Testament, where riches are sometimes seen as a sign of God's favor, but in the New Testament it is loud and clear.

Jesus lived a life of utter simplicity, drew his disciples mostly from the poor, shared a common purse with them, ate plain food, wore simple clothes, said that he had less of a home than a bird or a fox. "Do not lay up for yourselves treasures on earth," he taught. (Matthew 6:19) "Beware of all covetousness," he warned, "for a man's life does not consist in the abundance of his possessions." (Luke 12:15) "Sell your possessions," he commanded. (Luke 12:33) Do not be anxious about food or clothing. (Matthew 6:25–33) He proclaimed salvation to a house where a rich tax collector gave half of his goods to the poor. (Luke 19:1–11) Fascination with riches, he taught, can be one of the main barriers to hearing and understanding the deepest truth about life. (Matthew 13:22) "You cannot serve God and mammon," he stated bluntly. (Matthew 6:24)

Not only is the desire for riches condemned, but those who already *are* wealthy are described as barely able to enter the kingdom, if at all. (Matthew 19:23–26; Mark 10:23–27; Luke 18:24–27; cf. James 5:1–5) Their wealth is seen not as a source of security, but as a terrible spiritual burden, a barrier to their right relations with God and their fellow humans. The great possessions of the rich young man were viewed by Jesus as something preventing him from living life to the fullest. (Matthew 19:16–22) "How hard it will be for those who have riches to enter the kingdom of God," Jesus exclaims to the amazement of his disciples. (Mark 10:23) We can imagine how Jesus' poverty-stricken listeners must have responded to the story of the rich man "who was clothed in purple and fine linen," but who ended up in Hades, begging Abraham to warn his affluent brothers, while the poor Lazarus, whom he had ignored, was carried by angels to Abraham's bosom. (Luke 16:19–31)

SECTION II: ANOTHER WAY

A Lean, Simple Life in Community and in the Spirit

If the pursuit of wealth is roundly criticized, what is the alternative? Henry David Thoreau wrote that a person is rich in proportion to the number of things he or she can afford to leave alone.[12] In like manner, Jesus turns values topsy-turvy, teaching that the leader must be a servant, the great must be humble, the rich must be those of few possessions. (See Matthew 19:16–22; 20:20–28.)

Part of this different richness is spiritual. Jesus is seeking to remove the anxiety and the nervous grasping for more and more that leads a person to envy and dissatisfaction, and a society to oppression, imperialism, and war. (See James 4:1–3.) He is seeking to root us in an inner peace and security that, unlike possessions, cannot be taken away from us. (Matthew 6:19–21) He asks us to dwell in his words, his Spirit, and his shalom. (John 14:27, 15:4–10)

But part of the new richness is very concrete and human. When Jesus asked the rich young man to sell his goods and give to the poor, he did not say "Become destitute and friendless." Rather, he said, "Come, follow me." (Matthew 19:21) In other words, he invited him to join a community of sharing and love, where his security would not be based on individual property holdings, but on openness to the Spirit and on the loving care of new-found brothers and sisters. This is an extremely important point, for we often hear Jesus' demand that his disciples renounce possessions described as a "counsel of perfection," something not meant for most of us. But Jesus is not calling us to a poverty that would force us to spend every waking moment scratching for something to eat in wretched, lonely destitution. Jesus' disciples were poor, but out of love they shared and cared for one another.

After Jesus speaks the seemingly utopian and impractical words, "Do not be anxious about your life, what you shall eat or what you shall drink . . . Look at the birds of the air . . . Consider the lilies of the field," he says, "But seek first his kingdom and his righteousness, and all these things shall be yours as well." (Matthew 6:25, 26, 28, 33) What does he mean? The terms "kingdom" and "righteousness" are both social terms. A kingdom is a place ruled over by a king, and in Jesus' teachings, the king is God. But this king is love. Here, then, is a new way to find spiritual—and material—security. The way is not by laying up for *oneself* treasure on earth, not by individualistic accumulation, not by asking anxiously: "What shall *I* eat? What shall *I* wear?" The way is by building up and living in concrete human communities where love will so rule that the needs of all will be met. Indeed, this was the spirit of the early Christian community, where all things were held in common and goods were distributed on the basis of need. (Acts 2:44–45)

May we not glimpse in this Jesus' vision of a society whose members no longer see themselves struggling alone for security, but where food and drink and clothes are theirs because society is enough imbued with justice that it makes them available to all?

God Exalts the Poor and the Oppressed

The Bible does not stop with a call to the nonpoor to remember the needy. It also portrays God as achieving many of his purposes *through* the oppressed, the humble, the victimized.

Isaiah's vision of a suffering servant is of a person oppressed, afflicted, despised, and rejected. (Isaiah 53:3, 7) In the Beatitudes the poor and meek and persecuted inherit the kingdom. The apostle Paul writes that God chose the weak and despised to carry out his will, and he describes the brethren "as poor, yet making many rich; as having nothing, and yet possessing everything." (1 Corinthians 1:27–28; 2 Corinthians 6:10) And James asks: "Has not God chosen those who are poor in the world to be rich in faith and heirs of the kingdom which he has promised to those who love him?" (James 2:5)

We can expect that God will often seek his purposes through challenges to the economic status quo from those who suffer under it. In our time, the challenges come from such people in the United States as Blacks, Native Americans, Chicanos, and Appalachian whites. And in all times the challenges come from people in poor countries that are exploited by stronger nations.

New Motives in Human Relationships

Modern economics assumes that "economic man" will pursue his personal financial gain ahead of everything else. In the economic view, individual units compete against each other, seeking to maximize their income and to minimize their costs.

The Bible recognizes the reality of such human motivation, but a strong biblical theme is that a spirit of concern, cooperation, service, and economic sharing should be substituted for the motive of personal aggrandizement. "Through love be servants of one another." (Galatians 5:13) "Let no one seek his own good, but the good of his neighbor." (1 Corinthians 10:24) "Give to him who begs from you, and do not refuse him who would borrow from you." (Matthew 5:42) When Jesus washed his disciples' feet, it was to plant in their minds an image of humble service that would shape their relations (John 13:1–6), for "whoever would be great among you must be your servant." (Mark 10:43)

God's Ownership—Humans' Trusteeship—of the Earth

The motives of sharing and seeking for mutual well-being, along with the biblical sense of God's relation to the world he created, give a peculiar thrust to biblical ideas of property ownership. The Bible consistently gives stern warnings against the temptations and possible abuse of property ownership and the products (or "works") of human hands.

Modern Western economics tends to assume a high degree of private ownership of productive resources, such as land, factories, and machinery, The owner is given a relatively free hand in how these assets will be employed, including the right to accumulate from them unlimited amounts of personal wealth. A typical definition of capitalism says that it is "a system of economic organization in which individual persons, singly or in groups, privately own productive resources, including land, and possess the right to use these resources generally in whatever manner they choose."[13]

The basis of the restoration of property in the Jubilee Year, however, is that "the land belongs solely to God," a concept that forbids absolute human ownership.[14] "The land shall not be sold in perpetuity, for the land is mine." (Leviticus 25:23) "The earth is the Lord's and the fullness thereof." (Psalm 24:1)

In the Genesis account, God created the earth and set men and women in it to tend it according to God's will. When this is combined with the idea of the Divine Fatherhood, the earth is seen as being given to people in trust so that they will use its resources to sustain the human family.

These ideas suggest that God wants humans to look upon themselves as trustees of their possessions, property, and productive capital, seeking to use them in the light of their understanding of God's purposes.[15] At points in Christian history, and particularly in the life of the primitive church, this was interpreted to mean that property should be held and used in common, to assure that it would be made available for the common good rather than for individual aggrandizement (cf. Acts 2:44–45, 4:32–37, 5:1–6). This has led one modern theologian to write:

We need to regain the perspective of the Early Church, which accepted regulated possession and use as the best system, in which the means of production are held and used for the common good, and the necessities of consumption adequately provided for all.[16]

Seeking God's Kingdom

"The unifying theme of the Bible," says Old Testament scholar Robert C. Dentan, "is the kingdom of God—God's perfect and undisputed rule over all that he has created."[17] The exact wording, "kingdom of God," does not occur in the canonical books of the Old Testament, but the thought of God's kingship is used "to express the whole range of Israel's faith."[18]

For Jesus, of course, the term "kingdom of God" or "kingdom of heaven" is so central that he asks his followers to seek the kingdom before anything else and to pray "thy kingdom come, thy will be done, on earth." (Matthew 6:10,33)

The God of the kingdom is he who thunders in the words of the prophets, "Remove the evil of your doings from before my eyes . . . seek justice, correct oppression, defend the fatherless, plead for the widow" (Isaiah 1:16–17) and speaks tenderly in the Gospels, "Love one another as I have loved you." (John 15:12)

God's will is that his kingdom be realized on earth, among human beings, "and that his lordship be acknowledged over all principalities and powers, over every department of life, including economic institutions and practices."[19] From a biblical point of view, then, the basic criterion by which economic institutions are assessed is the rule of God—a rule under which economic injustice is righted, human material needs are met, persons are valued, equality of wealth is furthered, trusteeship is encouraged, and community is created in love and work for the common good.

Shalom

Much of what we have been discussing is caught up in the Hebrew word *shalom*, which is used repeatedly throughout the Old Testament. Shalom means not just peace, but unity, partnership, well-being, health, wholeness, community, and justice. It includes not only the right relations of people to one another but also the responsible relations of people to the natural world—plants, animals, earth, sea, and air.[20]

To be shalom means to be well, to have the needs of the body and the spirit gratified. The poor, the hungry, and the oppressed are deprived of their shalom . . . Shalom is thoroughly corporate and political, a social transaction of man in relation to his fellow man. ("Private shalom" is a contradiction in terms.) Shalom is possible where two or three are gathered and act together for the common good.[21]

The biblical vision of shalom functions always as a firm rejection of values and life-styles which seek security and well-being in manipulative ways at the expense of another part of creation, another part of the community, or another brother. The vision of the biblical way affirms that communal well-being comes by living God's dream and not by idolatrous self-aggrandizement.[22]

Injustice, including economic oppression, disrupts the shalom intended by God for humanity, and this brings turmoil and anxiety to human society. The pursuit of righteousness and justice helps to build a community of shalom.

Depart from evil and do good; seek shalom and pursue it.
—Psalm 34:14
Then justice will dwell in the wilderness, and righteousness in the fruitful field. And the effect of righteousness will be shalom, and the result of righteousness, quietness and trust forever.
—Isaiah 32:16–17

The Bible seems to portray the Creator of the universe as engaged in a long-term venture. He calls humans to participate in the creation of communities of shalom, looking toward the realization of a world community of shalom in which all people work for the well-being of the whole.

Implications for Christians

What does the recognition of these biblical themes mean in terms of our action as Christians in the world? What kind of economic order should Christians be working for and how should they go about their work?

Humility and Restraint: Modern history, with its war and racism, its totalitarian societies and concentration camps, its depressions and dashed hopes, has made us acutely aware of the power of evil in human life. This power is shown in tendencies toward egocentricity, greed, pride, and lust for power. It inhabits people's will, behavior, and institutions, and it easily undercuts and destroys human ability to achieve dreams of a better society.

The modern Christian theologian Reinhold Niebuhr has been at the forefront of the attack on any form of naive optimism, and has reminded us insistently of the biblical doctrine of sin—the self-centered intransigence of human nature that makes the achievement of social progress neither easy nor inevitable.

Any attempt to implement the biblical demand for justice and shalom in economic life, therefore, must be characterized by a restraint that recognizes the resistance of social institutions to change, that perceives the ambiguity of historical achievement, and that does not promise utopia as a result of human enterprise. As we struggle for economic justice, we must recognize the limiting effect of our *own* sin and finitude. We see things selectively. Our understanding is limited by upbringing, class, and culture. Our own self-centeredness distorts our ability to hear God's word and to act upon it. We cannot fully grasp the nature of God's kingdom or know with complete certainty what changes in society will be in accord with his will. What we call evil, God in his wisdom may call good, and vice versa. We have to look beyond our own power for the final and perfect fulfillment that only God can bring. When we speak of the future we must say with Gabriel Fackre: "Do not expect the kingdom to come in history. Evil grows with good. The anti-Christ appears in the last days."[23]

Another reason for restraint is that biblical themes, by

and large, do not give us specific and detailed answers to complicated modern economic problems. The biblical writers had no knowledge of modern industrial society, and there is no discussion in the Bible of the pros and cons of the negative income tax or of raising the Federal Reserve Board interest rate. There is no biblical judgment on capitalism, socialism, or communism because these political–economic systems did not even exist in biblical times.

In our approach to the solution of concrete modern economic problems, then, we cannot presume to have *the* biblical answer for every question. Where biblical guidelines are unclear, we will need to be guided by prudence and reason, keeping in mind biblical norms and spirit.

Prophetic Action: But we must not be daunted by the fact that it is necessary to approach the subject of economic justice with humility and restraint. Reinhold Niebuhr did not "discover" the Christian doctrine of sin. The biblical writers were utterly realistic about the stubbornness of human sin, and they describe its roots and effects from Genesis through Revelation. Yet this realization did not lock them pessimistically into an immovable social and economic status quo. Deeply recognizing human self-centeredness and the ambiguity of much human achievement, they still call people toward a vision of justice and wholeness, toward shalom.

Overwhelmed by the holiness of "the Lord, sitting upon a throne, high and lifted up," Isaiah knew himself to be lost, "a man of unclean lips . . . in the midst of a people of unclean lips." (See Isaiah 6:1–8.) Yet he found in the Lord, not only forgiveness for his sin, but also a voice asking, "Whom shall I send, and who will go for us?" And when he responded, "Send me," he found himself acting in entirely new ways and speaking fervently to his people, calling them, in the name of God, to a new level of societal justice and righteousness.

As Christians, we have to beware of the pretensions of superhuman self-righteousness, but we also have to avoid a subhuman lack of accountability. Sin is not only pride but also sloth—failure to assume responsibility, world weariness and timidity, indifference to the plight of suffering humanity, apathy in the face of injustice that still acts to "trample the head of the poor into the dust of the earth." (Amos 2:7) As Christians, we can have the freedom to speak out courageously for justice and social change, knowing the forgiveness that God in Christ makes available to us. In spite of our finitude, some evils are so great, some oppressions so contrary to the biblical message, that we need to cry out boldly, with prophetic indignation, against their being continued at all. In spite of our sin, God invites, urges, implores us to participate in his project of creating just societies and loving communities. And, when we respond, he is there in his Spirit, not only to forgive our failures but also to grant us power to move mountains of injustice and to find new depths of love.

Indeed, it is a rather sorry kind of love that is indifferent to oppression. If we know anything of the love of God, we should be moved to "seek justice, correct oppression, defend the fatherless, plead for the widow." (Isaiah 1:17) If God has inspired in us any real love for our neighbors, we should want to work for a society in which children no longer have to suffer hunger and poverty. "To love thy neighbor," said a recent statement of Chilean priests, "means to struggle to make this world resemble the future world we await."[24]

The biblical themes and stories may not give us prescriptions for every contemporary economic ill, but they do provide a powerful context in which to judge modern economic practices. The Bible, though written millennia ago, has a powerful contemporary ring. Then, as now, the poor are being crushed and needs are going unmet because of human greed. Then, as now, institutions are considered more important than human beings. Then, as now, loving communities do more to encourage human fulfillment and happiness than do competitive, individualistic ones. Whereas it is true that historical achievement is ambiguous and that no perfect utopia is built by human effort, there *is* a difference, in God's eyes, between a society in which crushing poverty exists side by side with immense wealth and one in which everyone has a minimal decent life—between a society in which only the rich receive adequate health care and one in which everyone has such care.

The Bible does not show us a way forward without sin, but it does show us a way forward—to a society more in harmony with God's coming kingdom. Guided by it, we cannot create institutions that are themselves identical to the kingdom, but we can oppose those that are hostile to its spirit and that make the rule of God less real. We can struggle against what blocks shalom—injustice, oppression, hatred, greed, structures and attitudes that fail to meet human needs. And we can support what makes for shalom. We can work to build attitudes and institutions that are more open to the love and justice of the kingdom and that make the expression of its spirit more real on earth.

Understanding, Hope, and Action

In summary, then, how should we strive for economic justice?

First is to understand as deeply as possible our present economic arrangements and their social–political context. This means in-depth study of the actual impact of the economy on human beings and of any contradictions between biblical values and the operation of the economy. Knowledge is an essential basis for meaningful action.

Second is to develop a vision of what the God of justice and shalom calls on our society to do and to be in this moment in time. Because of sin and finitude, this will always be a tentative vision, but reflection on God's purposes in the Bible, combined with a growing knowledge of the realities of contemporary life, will help to deepen the vision of how our economic life could be more just, less oppressive, more equal, more loving.[25] Because God is at work in all nations, one way to help develop vision is to study how other countries are grappling with problems of equality, injustice, and human need. Such study will often shed light on the concrete potential of human beings to achieve a measure of shalom in their economic life. Creative imagination, too, informed by the biblical spirit, can open up new possibilities and point to better ways of organizing economic life.

Third is to try to sense how God would have us work and act with him to transform values, attitudes, and institutions so that they may be more harmonious with his coming kingdom. At the same time, we should acknowledge that he is leading the way, working for shalom among the poor and the oppressed.

Implications for Our Economic Life Today

If the above says something about how Christians may work for humanizing change, can we be more specific about the kind of economic order that biblical faith seems to call for in the modern world?

Each person has to decide, prayerfully and thoughtfully, for himself and with others the meaning for today of the biblical themes of justice, concern for the needy, human dignity, familyhood, work, equality, simplicity of possessions, community, service, trusteeship, and shalom. In the pages to come, we will be searching for the application of biblical themes to the American economic order. We will look first at some pros and cons of the United States economy, then at ways of working for economic justice, and finally at several critical areas where there is a need for major change.

Questions for Discussion

1. Do you find disparities between current economic issues and your religious faith?

2. What was the prophet Isaiah referring to when he spoke of "grinding the face of the poor"? (Isaiah 3:15) Do poor people endure similar treatment today? How is their treatment related to the question of economic justice?

3. What do the Fatherhood of God and the brotherhood and sisterhood of the human family imply for us in the way we earn and spend our incomes?

4. Study the scripture passage about the rich young man (Matthew 19:21). What was his problem, and what was Jesus' solution? At what point did riches become a problem for this man?

5. What biblical themes, in addition to those in this chapter, bear on the question of economic justice?

6. Does the Bible suggest an "economic vision" that points beyond our present economic reality to one that you think may be better?

Suggested Reading

Alves, Rubem. *A Theology of Human Hope*. Washington, D.C.: Corpus Books, 1969. A young Brazilian theologian critiques much of modern religious thought and develops theology from a "Third World" point of view.

DeWolf, L. Harold. *Responsible Freedom*. New York: Harper & Row, 1971. Social, political, and economic implications of the Christian faith.

Heschel, Abraham J. *The Prophets*. New York: Harper & Row, 1963. A provocative study of the Hebrew prophets, with implications for the present.

Kirk, David. *Quotations from Chairman Jesus*. New York: Bantam Books, 1969. The biblical message related to today's social issues.

Moltmann, Jürgen. *Religion, Revolution and the Future*. Translated by Douglas Meeks. New York: Charles Scribner's Sons, 1969. Many of today's social problems viewed from the perspective of a modern "theology of hope."

Paupert, Jean Marle. *The Politics of the Gospel*. New York: Holt, Rinehart & Winston, 1969. A French Catholic priest argues that the gospel has profound political and economic implications.

Rauschenbusch, Walter. *Theology for the Social Gospel*. New York: Macmillan Co., 1917. A challenging application of theology to the social scene—provocative reading in spite of its publishing date.

Ruether, Rosemary. *The Radical Kingdom*. New York: Harper & Row, 1970. A lay Catholic theologian shows the historical involvement of Christians in struggles for political and economic justice.

Tillich, Paul. *Political Expectation*. Edited by James Luther Adams. New York: Harper & Row, 1971. Early political essays of the Protestant theologian, Paul Tillich.

CHAPTER 2

The Economic Structures of the United States

SECTION I: AN ASSESSMENT

There are people today who completely despair of the economic structure of the United States. There are others who champion it as the best economic system in the world. Discussion of economic structures is often caught between what John Gardner has called "unloving critics" and "uncritical lovers." When criticism appears below, it is offered by a "critical lover," one who sees great potential in this country and wants it to be a blessing to the world.

Good Things

There are attitudes, practices, and institutions associated with the United States economy that, potentially or in actuality, seem supportive of biblical values. Below is a list of what I consider these to be.

• People from other lands, who have been oppressed and locked into poverty, have found this country to be a haven from persecution and a place where they can find education and economic opportunity to build "the good life" according to their own desires.

• Crucial personal and political freedoms function, in spite of forces attempting to undercut them. Our economic system has developed, on the whole, without the elimination of such civil rights as freedom of worship; access to information; and freedom to publish and disseminate ideas, to organize labor unions, and to associate and organize for political and social change. These freedoms, and the rights on which they are based, have sometimes been limited (political dissenters and minority groups such as Blacks or Native Americans have known these limitations), but their expression is possible in this society where people value the dignity of the human person.

• An emphasis on acquisitiveness and competition has not eliminated respect for the principles of equal opportunity, justice, fair play, human dignity, democracy, and conscience. There is sympathy for the underdog, for people suffering through no fault of their own, for the little guy who is unfairly pushed around. Millions of Americans each year give to charities to aid the sick and those less fortunate than themselves. There is a significant number of Americans who still dream about, and work for, a more just, equitable, and democratic society.

• Part of the American ethos is to meet one's responsibility to society through productive work. This sometimes has led to insensitivitiy and even callousness toward those not able to work. But the commitment to responsible labor, when combined with vast technological developments, has built an immense productive capacity for meeting the material needs of large numbers of people. This productivity has laid the basis for expenditures to aid the sick, the disabled, the unemployed, the aged, and those suffering from natural or human-made disasters.

• The economic system has stimulated scientific advance and has created a complex technology, at least part of which can be useful in solving many of the problems now faced by humanity. It has released much creativity, energy, and ingenuity to solve problems, to make life more enjoyable, to make work easier and more productive. It is an innovative and experimental system, open to the new, the untried, the unexplored, and flexibly adaptable to the many changes that keep sweeping in upon the world. It has been open to social progress, some examples of which are the elimination of child labor in factories and the passage of pure food and drug laws.

• It has created networks of cooperation and mutual aid through thousands of cooperative enterprises in such fields as food retailing, housing, telephone service, rural electricity, credit, farm equipment, and medical services. Membership in cooperatives in the United States now totals more than fifty million people. About twenty-four million people in the United States now save money through some 23,000 cooperative credit unions. (For example, farmer friends of mine from Kansas, who are members of a rural electrical cooperative, read their own electric meters and make up their own bills.)

• The economic system has made room at the national, state, and local levels for a large public sector, which furnishes services and facilities such as roads, education, water supply, medical research, public health, libraries, old age pensions, parks, and housing.

But Something Has Gone Wrong

• Americans who watched the CBS documentary, "Hunger in America," on May 21, 1968, were shocked to watch on their television screens an American Indian baby taking its last struggling breaths, and dying of starvation, while a doctor tried desperately to revive it.

During that same year, specialists familiar with food deficiency and starvation carried out the United States government-authorized National Nutrition Survey and expressed astonishment at finding conditions in the United States similar to those in Asia, Africa, and Latin America, including cases of kwashiorkor, a starvation disease formerly associated only with "backward" countries.[1]

In that same year, the Citizens' Board of Inquiry into Hunger and Malnutrition in the United States, a group of prominent doctors, nutritionists, clergy, college presidents, and civic leaders, released their report, Hunger, U.S.A. After extensive scientific research, hearings, and field trips to many parts of the country, they concluded that at least ten million people in the United States suffer from hunger and malnutrition, and that the problem is "increasing in severity and extent from year to year."[2] Hunger sometimes means starvation and death, they said. More often it means constant pain, low resistance and increased susceptibility to disease, stunted growth and possible brain damage, sickness in mothers leading to deaths in childbirth, inability to learn, lethargy and exhaustion at work, and resentment at life. The report pointed out that governmental efforts, such as food stamps and school lunch programs, have failed miserably in meeting the needs of the hungry poor. The massive private food industry showed little or no interest in the unprofitable problem of feeding the poor and, in fact, worked against legislation to provide food for the hungry.[3]

The pace of public interest built up when Senator Ernest F. Hollings, of South Carolina, admitted in Senate testimony that there is "substantial hunger" in his home state and that state pride and the desire for industrial development had "resulted in a public policy of covering up hunger."[4] Other senators and members of Congress agreed, pointing out that hunger and malnutrition are to be found in all fifty states.

For a while there was widespread interest in the plight of the hungry. Art Buchwald wrote a perceptive column, "Farewell to Poverty, Hail to Hunger."[5] "Hunger planks" appeared in both the Republican and Democratic platforms. Members of Congress made "hunger trips." A White House Conference on Food Nutrition and Health was called. The Coalition to Help Malnourished Americans and similar groups were organized. *The New York Times* ran a series on hunger, and top magazines carried articles. Senator George McGovern said, "To admit the existence of hunger in America is to confess that we have failed in meeting the most sensitive and painful of human needs."[6] President Richard Nixon stated: "That hunger and malnutrition should persist in a land such as ours is embarrassing and intolerable . . . Something like the very honor of American democracy is involved."[7]

"How is it possible," people asked, "for starvation to occur in the world's richest nation, where 'the food problem' is usually thought of in terms of overweight people looking for the perfect diet or the Federal government paying farmers to cut back on troublesome food surpluses?"

But this widespread interest was not sustained. Four years later, in 1972, the Citizens' Board brought out an updated report, *Hunger, U.S.A. Revisited,* which shows that, in spite of increased public concern and larger Federal expenditures, the hunger problem is still in crisis proportions. The report charges that half the nation's poor are still going hungry and receive no help whatsoever from governmental food programs. The hunger problem, says the report, "has been officially acknowledged, described and defined, and left unsolved."[8]

Robert Heilbroner, in *The Economic Problem,* states as "the imperious first rule of continued existence" that "the human being must eat"; and he describes economics as a study of "the process of providing for the material well-being of society . . . the study of how man earns his daily bread."[9] The Declaration of Independence lists at the head of our "inalienable rights" the right to life. Has something happened to this basic right in an economy that fails to meet the needs of millions of Americans for the most basic and fundamental factor of life—nourishing food?

It is this kind of reality that caused the Reverend Jesse Jackson, a well-known Black civil rights leader, to comment: "There is inherent evil in a system that induces men to plow crops under while others starve."[10] How do these economic factors compare with those the prophet Jeremiah said make a people "grow fat and sleek" but "not defend the rights of the needy"? (Jeremiah 5:28) What do we say to the Lord before whom will be gathered all the nations of the world to be judged first and foremost on whether they fed the hungry and gave drink to the thirsty? (Matthew 25:31 ff.)

That there should be painful, crippling hunger for millions of people in a land with a trillion dollar gross national product is enough to give pause to any sensitive person. But there are other economics-linked realities the existence of which raises profound questions about the ability of our economic system, as presently structured, to express anything approaching the biblical vision of shalom.

• Poverty is the condition for more than twenty-five million Americans, one in eight people, including one-sixth of the nation's children.[11] Unemployment has been in the millions for over two decades, and unemployment compensation benefits are below the poverty level in all but a few states.[12] As a recent Presidential Commission admitted:

"Millions of persons in our society . . . eke out a bare existence under deplorable conditions."[13] The original intention of giving people freedom to grow and develop, to use their work to carve sustenance out of the wilderness, is not adequate to overcome poverty in an urbanized, industrialized society.

• We have wanted to promote equality of opportunity, but vast inequality of incomes and assets persists. Some people receive close to no income from the economy, while nine out of ten executives of top corporations "have income before taxes ranging from $100,000 to over $1 million."[14] Many people have negative assets, because of the burden of debt, while the rich accumulate wealth in the multimillions of dollars. "Surfeit of food and prosperous ease" (Ezekiel 16:49) exist side by side with misery and stark human need.

• The economy can easily produce estates for the wealthy, but too often it provides only rotting slums for the poor. The building industry has never found a way to produce low-cost housing to meet the needs of low-income people. As stated in the 1969 report of the President's Council of Economic Advisors:

Investing in new housing for low-income families—particularly in big cities—is usually a losing proposition. Indeed, the most profitable investment is in the demolition of homes of low-income families to make room for business and higher-income families.[15]

Governmental programs, such as urban renewal and code enforcement, ostensibly designed to help the poor, have, according to a Presidential Commission, "destroyed more housing for the poor than government at all levels has built for them."[16]

• Poverty is compounded by racism and discrimination; which lock Blacks into poverty, keep Black unemployment twice as high as white, and have a similar oppressing effect on other minorities—arbitrarily excluding them from jobs, housing, and other benefits of the economy. Discrimination also inhibits women's participation in the economy,

and results in lack of job opportunities and unequal pay
for equal work. The aged suffer disproportionate poverty
(one out of every six Americans over age 65 lives in poverty) and often feel cast off by the rest of society.

• The priorities of the economy go toward military hard-
ware and toward encouraging the private sector, while
public needs, such as mass transit and public education,
go unmet. Military programs consume tremendous amounts
of industrial resources and research talent. Over one half
of Federal taxes go toward paying for wars—past, present,
and future.

• Billions are spent on health care, providing doctors
with a median annual income of over $40,000[17] but with
highly unequal results in terms of treatment. The United
States is one of the few modern developed countries that
still treats its medical system like a private business. Good
medical care is not regarded as a human right, but as a
commodity to be purchased. Excellent care can be had
by those who have the money, but it is barely available
to those who do not. Private medical insurance meets
some costs, but one in five Americans has no such cover-
age. Most insurance that *is* available does not cover all
medical costs. The situation is reflected in our relative
standing in world health indexes: the United States ranks
about eighteenth in the world in infant mortality rates, just
ahead of Hong Kong.[18]

My wife is a nurse, and she can never forget the screams
of poor people in the clinics of hospitals where she has
worked. She remembers well the young Puerto Rican
woman crying out in the delivery room, "Dios Mío, Dios
Mío, ayudame, ayudame" (My God, My God, help me,
help me) as an inexperienced doctor performed two sur-
gical incisions without anesthesia. When my wife pro-
tested, she was told that clinic patients do not get a choice
of anesthesia whereas, of course, private patients do.
"And behold, the tears of the oppressed, and they had no
one to comfort them!" (Ecclesiastes 4:1)

• Economic institutions tend to be judged not by
whether they meet human needs but by whether they realize profits and growth. The pursuit of private wealth is

prized and lauded, rather than held suspect, and the values of love, service, and sharing as motives in economic life are viewed as unrealistic. Advertising continually stimulates the desire to accumulate more and more material goods, and millions are spent each year to develop psychological techniques for making people dissatisfied with what they have and eager to acquire more. Advertising teaches that a person's life *does* consist in the abundance of one's possessions (see Luke 12:15). Competition sets person against person, group against group, and undercuts the sense of each person's being a member of the human family, called to work for the good of all.

• There is no basic security for the aged, the injured, the unemployed, or the sick (for security facts, see page 51 ahead). Pensions, social security, unemployment compensation, and welfare payments have all proved woefully inadequate to meet the needs of those who lose earning capacity through no fault of their own.[19] Not only the poor but middle-class people too suffer anxiety over whether high medical bills will wipe out a lifetime's savings or whether a change of job or a company's bankruptcy will eliminate a pension program needed for security in old age.

• Middle- and working-class people are plagued by rising pollution, inflation, unsafe automobiles, crime, consumer fraud, and job monotony. They are angry at paying taxes, knowing of the many loopholes available to the wealthy and the way wealth is used to buy votes and to undercut democratic political processes. Workers find themselves treated as "factors of production" rather than as persons, and often they feel that they have no share in the decisions that affect their lives.

• The economy seems incapable of ending ecological destruction, and industry continues to use up irreplaceable resources while destroying lakes and rivers and polluting earth and air. A recent Federal study found 665,000 square miles of the Atlantic Ocean fouled by chemical debris, apparently due, at least in part, to pollution from oil tankers and chemical factories.[20] The drive toward ever-increasing economic growth is pushing against the possibility of ecocide—the suicide of the human race because of the poisoning of the fragile ecosystem on which all life depends.

• Not only is the economy careless of the needs of its own people, but economic practices overseas often result in propping up unpopular dictatorships, inhibiting third world development, and making the rich grow richer as the poor get poorer. (For documentation, see pages 98 to 101.) Much of our affluent society is dependent on the extraction of the resources of other lands.

In the chapters ahead, we will be searching for ways in which Christians can work on behalf of what makes for shalom in our economic life and in opposition to the forces and practices that prevent its realization.

SECTION II: WORKING FOR ECONOMIC JUSTICE

Where is it most crucial to work for economic justice in our present society? One approach is to deal with those aspects of our economy that are particularly oppressive and unjust and that make it harder for people to respond to God's call for shalom. Key questions to ask are:

1. What biblical insights are relevant to the oppressive and unjust aspects of our economic life?
2. What is the present-day reality in this dimension of the economic system?
3. Is there a better way to organize economic life—an alternative that gives more hope of ending exploitation, meeting human needs, and enabling people to work together for the common good?
4. How may we work on behalf of this better way?

This is the posture of "understanding, hope, and action" that was mentioned at the end of the chapter, "A Theology of Economic Justice." It is a simple method that all of us often use to solve problems in much less complex areas of life: (1) understanding the problem, (2) exploring alternative solutions, and (3) applying solutions.

Alternative Solutions

The question of alternatives is difficult. Almost anyone can point out an existing problem such as slums or pollution, but no one can say with certainty that an alternative approach will be better than the present one. Yet we are impelled to search for alternatives because of our sense that much of the human suffering that now occurs is avoidable. Our biblical study suggests that God calls us, not only to be aware of human degradation, but to work for more concrete embodiments of justice and love.

In the pages to come, therefore, there will be no pat solutions or easy answers. We will look hard, however, for anything that suggests a better way forward. Some suggestions will come from present American experience and from thinkers who have reflected on how our economy might be made more humane. Some will come from the experience of other nations.

There are those who argue that we cannot learn anything of value from other countries. I agree that other nations have different conditions, and what they have done may not work here. I have no illusions that any other countries have achieved utopia. But I also agree with Warren Burger, Chief Justice of the United States Supreme Court, who said:

Immature societies, like immature people, sometimes tend to think that everything they have is "the best": but we are now the oldest continuing republic on earth and we have no need to bolster our national ego. We can afford to take a hard look at all our institutions, to compare them with other societies, and to learn from them as they have so often learned from us.[21]

If we acknowledge that there are alternatives, whether drawn from our own experience or that of other nations, how can we work to achieve them? Anyone can produce a shopping list of "good things to do," but the trick is to avoid palliatives and Band-aids and to find the actions that have the best chance of causing major positive changes leading to major positive improvements. Problems of the magnitude we have been discussing cannot be solved by some minor readjustments in institutions or by passing a few new laws. When millions are hungry, when appalling poverty affects one in every eight Americans, when wealth coexists comfortably with staggering need, when national priorities focus on weapons of destruction rather than institutions of healing, when the ecosystem is on the verge of shattering; then major change is called for in our attitudes, behavior, and institutions.

Social Problems Require Social Solutions

Some will argue that the role of Christians is not to work for large-scale social changes, but to try to change people's hearts and minds. Certainly a continuing crucial role of Christians is to work for personal commitment to the spirit and teachings of Christ and to encourage those personal qualities of character that flow from life in Christ. But we cannot climb our private ladders to heaven and forget the whole world with its misery and sadness.

The need to work for social justice and social change was made vividly clear to me in an article by a Presbyterian minister, Richard G. Watts, "Social Injustice Often Makes Personal Goodness Irrelevant." The author referred to Hitler's persecution of the Jews, who were robbed and beaten and finally sent to concentration camps. He then describes a "personal goodness" response:

You yourself were not anti-Semitic, and did not approve of minority group persecution. You had your Jewish neighbors in to dinner, listened with them to Mozart, and played on the living-room rug with their children. But if you did not protest against the public policy which made them wear armbands, defrauded them of property, and shipped them off to death, your little kindnesses were of no importance whatever. Your personal decency could never make up for public persecution that dehumanized your neighbors and, indeed, destroyed them . . . The point is clear: personal goodness alone can never heal the ugly wounds inflicted by social injustice. The social structures themselves must be changed.[22]

The point is not that the United States is like Nazi Germany but that social problems require broad social solutions, as do the vast problems associated with our economic system.

Questions for Discussion

1. How do economic and social conditions today square with the Bible's stress on social and economic justice? Are there crucial respects in which the United States economy allows and even creates conditions that are contrary to the biblical vision of shalom?
2. If a biblical prophet were to walk through our nation today, would not he or she make many of the same fiery judgments about injustice, oppression, and an uncaring attitude toward the poor that he or she made millennia ago in the Near East?
3. With which of the "good things" about the United States economic system in this chapter do you agree? Why or why not? What would you add?
4. To what extent does our economic system create the injustices and social problems described in this section? Are other institutions, behaviors, or values also to blame?
5. Is it possible to overcome hunger, poverty, inequality, and ecological destruction within the framework of our present economic values and institutions? How far-reaching must the changes be in order to have a system that supports human dignity and meets desperate needs?
6. How much of what we buy stems from advertising pressures rather than from a rational assessment of real need?
7. To what extent do you feel economically secure? How would you handle a major illness with high hospital, drug, and doctors' fees?

Suggested Readings

The literature on the United States economic system and on economics-related social problems is vast. The books and articles below are well worth reading, but the list is not meant to be complete or representative of everything in the field.

Citizens' Board of Inquiry into Hunger and Malnutrition in the United States. *Hunger, U.S.A.* Washington, D.C.: New Community Press, 1968.

Galbraith, John K. *The New Industrial State.* New York: Houghton, 1967. A Harvard economist's view of the economic system of the United States.

Heilbroner, Robert L. "Benign Neglect in the United States," *Transaction 7* (October 1970): 15–22. How the United States compares with other countries in tackling problems such as unemployment, poverty, and health, and why we often do so poorly relative to others.

Kotz, Nick. *Let Them Eat Promises: The Politics of Hunger in America.* Englewood Cliffs, N.J.: Prentice-Hall, 1969. The tragic story of hunger in America and our failure to end it.

Lens, Sidney. *Poverty: America's Enduring Paradox.* New York: Thomas Y. Crowell, 1969. The various manifestations of poverty in America and why it has been with us for so long.

Lichtman, Richard. *Toward Community: A Critique of Contemporary Capitalism.* Santa Barbara, Calif.: Center for the Study of Democratic Institutions, 1966. The author argues that the very nature of our economic institutions produces the intractable problems we face.

Melman, Seymour. "Ten Propositions on the War Economy," *The American Economic Review* 62 (May, 1972): 312–18. The immense power and prerogatives of the American military.

Voorhis, Horace Jeremiah. *American Cooperatives.* New York: Harper & Bros., 1961. The inspiring story of the American cooperative movement.

CHAPTER 3

Justice and Human Need

SECTION I: WHAT IS AND WHAT MIGHT BE

Biblical Perspective

The God pictured in the Bible is profoundly concerned about human exploitation, injustice, and oppression and the hurt and suffering that flow from them. He is partial to the poor and the downtrodden and is indignant over their ill-treatment: "What do you mean by crushing my people, by grinding the face of the poor?" (Isaiah 3:15) He identifies himself with those who are hungry, thirsty, and in want, and feels their affliction as his own.

He works to save the victims of oppression, "to set at liberty those who are oppressed." (Luke 4:18) He calls upon humans to regard one another as members of a family and as such to "defend the rights of the needy" (Jeremiah 5:28), to "satisfy the desire of the afflicted" (Isaiah 58:10), to "let the oppressed go free" (Isaiah 58:6), and to create communities in which there is "not a needy person" (Acts 4:34), because a caring spirit produces institutions designed to serve the common good.

Today's Reality

Roman Catholic prelate John Cardinal Krol of Philadelphia spoke at the 1972 "Christmas at the White House" services in Washington.

For us to profess faith in God without hastening to eliminate the indignities inflicted upon men would be but empty rhetoric. . . . For us to profess the love of God without manifesting concern for the poor, the weak and the lonely would be a caricature of religion.[1]

In 1968, a few blocks from the White House, many of us slogged through the mud of the Poor People's Campaign's "Resurrection City," joining a few thousand poor people in their desperate plea to government and nation to respond to their plight. How much "empty rhetoric" has flowed since the police tear-gassed their way down the historic Mall, between the great American symbols of the Washington Monument and the Lincoln Memorial, to chase the poor people out of Martin Luther King's last project!

How can we grasp the anguish under which the needy and the afflicted live in the United States of today? Poverty in this country affects not just a few people, but a population as large as that of California, Oregon, and Washington combined: over twenty-five million people, by conservative estimate.

Poverty means never having enough. It means poor food, limited education, abysmal housing. It means hanging the baby's crib from the ceiling so the rats can't crawl up from the floor and bite him. It means living in fear— fear of sickness with no insurance to cover the bills, fear of the landlord with his evictions and rent hikes, fear of the high-interest finance company, fear of what old age will bring. It means not being able to meet the needs of your children—having to watch them play in the garbage-littered streets, enticed by gangs and junkies. It is always being overcrowded and uncomfortable, cold in the winter and sweltering in the summer. It is being looked upon as dumb, lazy, not fully human, suspected of being immoral or criminal. It is feeling humiliated and helpless in the face of forces beyond one's control.

This poverty cannot be overcome by personal effort or by following the model of the immigrants of the 1800's and leaving for the promised land. Poverty then, as bad as it was, was surrounded by hope—the realistic hope that the expanding economy could absorb vast amounts of muscle power, that the burgeoning trade union movement would win more benefits for the workers, that the vast lands of the frontier (made available cheaply to thousands of people through the Homestead Act of 1862) could be farmed and could lay the basis for self-sufficiency. But today an increasingly automated economy has less and less room for unskilled and semiskilled workers; the unions (which never drew in more than one-third of the labor force) are losing members; and the frontier is no more. And we have the continuing problem of racism and discrimination, locking minorities into ghettos and reservations, erecting walls against employment opportunities, limiting the education needed to compete in an increasingly technical economy.

Sometimes it is said that people are poor because they are lazy. But how can people look down on the poor as malingerers when faced with the reality of discrimination, the decrease in jobs for the unskilled and semiskilled and the paucity of training programs to educate them, the fact that one in every three persons classed as poor is a child under fourteen, the rise and fall in unemployment due to the business cycle (do we suddenly have several hundred thousand fewer lazy people when unemployment falls from 5 percent to 4 percent?), the more than one million poor who are too ill or too disabled to work, the poor (almost one-fourth of their number) who are working, but at jobs with pay so low that they are still in poverty?[2]

To avoid being poor, people must be able to work at a nonpoverty pay level and not have inflation eat away all their gains. But our economy is inflation-prone; it maintains an unemployment rate that keeps millions out of the job market all of the time; and it sets wage levels that make millions more into "working poor." It has been estimated that 60 percent of all poverty in the United States is attributable to unemployment or to employment at substandard wages.[3]

To avoid being poor, people need security of income, and help when they are unable to work because they are sick or disabled or too old. But, as the President's Commission on Income Maintenance Programs noted, "There is no overall system of economic security" in the United States.[4] Present programs of workmen's compensation, according to a report by a National Commission in July, 1972, to President Nixon, are "inadequate and inequitable," with fifteen percent of the labor force, who "usually are those most in need of protection," not even covered by any form of compensation.[5]

Retirement pensions provided by private companies are similarly inadequate, covering only one half of the private work force and giving less than $1,000 per year retirement income to more than one half of those who are covered by plans.[6] Welfare and Social Security, which should provide a "floor" of income for those unable to work, do not even reach many of the poor and provide only minimal, poverty-level incomes for many of those who are covered. This inadequacy is especially hard on the growing group of elderly, 86 percent of whom have chronic conditions, diseases, or impairments, and whose average income drops sharply after reaching age 65. Thirty percent of all older Americans live in substandard housing.[7] Over three million elderly live below the government's "poverty line" of $2,100 for a single elderly person, and $2,640 for a couple.[8] To show the impact of Social Security, when a 20 percent increase in payments took effect in October, 1972, the proportion of elderly in poverty dropped from about 25 percent (one in four impoverished) to about 17 percent.[9]

To avoid being poor, people need adequate housing and a decent living environment. But, as noted earlier, the private housing industry provides virtually no housing for the poor. A government study showed that the Federal urban renewal program removed 3.5 housing units—mainly through demolition—for every one it erected. And these houses were mainly for lower-income groups.[10]

In the early 1960's I worked for five years as executive director of a private housing agency in a large city. I saw that housing for the poor was torn down for urban renewal without adequate provision for relocation assistance. There was no real alternative to crowding into some other slum. (Six thousand people were on the waiting list for public housing.) Large areas were demolished and left vacant for years while other areas were rebuilt with housing priced far out of the reach of former residents. Although unable to help the poor, urban renewal did find it possible to provide $40,000 and up for townhouses for the wealthy in an historic part of the city called "Society Hill." Vast sums of taxpayers' dollars have been spent in programs of downtown renewal, making new buildings and other amenities available to central city banks and business corporations.

To avoid being poor, people need to get medical care when they are sick or injured (or on a preventive basis to keep them from getting sick) and not have the payments wipe out all of their savings. But, as Senator Edward Kennedy of Massachusetts and others have pointed out, medical costs are increasing dramatically, while quality is declining. We now trail many other nations in such crucial health indexes as life expectancy and the number of mothers who die in childbirth. With high health costs and insurance that does not cover many medical expenses, sickness can mean financial ruin.

"The average American citizen," said Senator Kennedy, "lives in dread of illness and disability . . . He lives in fear of the cost of health care."[11]

Our failure to respond adequately to the needs of the afflicted has repercussions far beyond the poor themselves. Everyone in the United States knows that the abyss of poverty lies below them. They know that life involves risk, and that there are no effective communal or governmental mechanisms to spread the risk and prevent a fall into destitution. Somewhere in our history, most of us have lost the feeling of security that comes from knowing that someone will take us in and not demand payment for his or her help if we encounter financial disaster. By emphasizing independence and rugged individualism, we have isolated ourselves from the help of a community of interdependence.

Everyone, therefore, must assume his or her own risks and try to accumulate enough income and assets to meet the looming potential expenses of housing, food, sickness, and old age. And, because the potential expenses are endless (imagine the cost of long-term hospitalization and major surgery!) people are constantly encouraged to grasp for more and more, never being sure that they will have "enough."

Because many of us have assumed that the economic conditions cannot be changed, we have heeded counsel (often religious) to be patient, to bear up, to accept the inevitable. But these conditions are not inevitable. In fact, many have been overcome in other countries.

What Are the Alternatives?

In the United States, a concerned person can spend many hours trying to figure out how a poor person may struggle up out of poverty. When a group of us made a study trip to Scandinavia, we found ourselves trying to figure out how people can *fall into* poverty if they want to. How can they escape the net of welfare benefits, free training programs, pensions, housing subsidies, and free medical plans that keep propping them up every time they start to fall? Jokingly, we went on "poverty hunts" to see if we could find any slums, any pockets of poverty. Finally, we did find some bad housing in two large cities, but it was nothing like the massive blight of slums in the United States. Stark poverty, as we experience it here, was nowhere to be seen.

Of course the Scandinavian countries, like all others, have their problems, one of which is, for example, Sweden's stress on materialistic values. But I was staggered, as we studied their prisons, their medical care, and their new towns, to see how much further advanced they were in these areas than the United States.

Medical Care: Sweden's medical system, for example, has given the country one of the lowest infant mortality rates in the world and the highest life expectancy for both men and women. The guiding principle is that the entire population should have the medical care it needs as a matter of right and without regard to the individual's ability to pay. Under the Swedish national health insurance system, everyone pays health insurance premiums along with his or her income tax. Out of this fund, hospital care is provided completely without charge, and this includes all treatment—tests, blood transfusions, drugs, and the most complicated and costly surgery. Everyone, with low or high income, can receive this same fine, high-quality care based solely on individual medical needs.

A person who is sick but not in need of hospitalization can go to a doctor of his or her choice. If one chooses a government-employed physician, he or she receives all treatment for the minimal fee of $1.50. If one goes to a private doctor (one-half of Swedish physicians are in private practice), she pays the doctor's fee, but upon presentation of the receipt to the local health insurance office, he is reimbursed for three-fourths of the cost.

Comprehensive dental care—including periodontics, oral surgery, and orthodontics—is provided free of charge for all school children up to age fifteen. If a Swede is disabled by an accident, he or she is entitled (in addition to free hospital care) to three free wheelchairs—one for work, one for outdoors, and one for the home. If a disabled person needs to adapt his or her home (e.g., installing ramps, lowering a sink to wheelchair level, etc.), a government grant is available to help.

The Swedish approach is not perfect. There are complaints about long waits for elective surgery, for example, and the total health system is not as comprehensive as those of some other nations. But it does seem to be characterized by the insistence that no citizen shall be without medical care due to lack of money. And, interestingly enough, Sweden spends proportionately less of its national income for its medical system than does the United States. Sweden gets a better system for less money.[12]

Unemployment: To turn to the problem of poverty-creating joblessness, it is an enlightening experience to pick up the *United Nations Statistical Yearbook* and to compare recent unemployment statistics cross-nationally. United States unemployment, year by year, almost always stands above 4 percent. But, countries such as Finland, Germany, the Netherlands, Norway, Britain, and Sweden nearly always have rates under 3 percent. Between 1960 and 1965, when the United States was experiencing an average unemployment of about 5½ percent, the rate in the Netherlands and in the Federal Republic of Germany never went over 1.2 percent.[13]

These low rates are not accidental, but are the result of careful planning and conscious policy. In Sweden we met with an official of the Royal Labor Market Board, the government agency charged with keeping unemployment to an absolute minimum. The Board attempts to guarantee to every Swede who is able and willing to work the right to employment in one job of his or her choice. When government fiscal and monetary policy is insufficient to generate enough jobs for those who need them, the Board, which runs employment offices throughout the country, takes measures to *create* jobs in the private or public sector and to retrain workers at whatever scale is necessary.

When an unemployed worker comes to the employment office, the policy is that he or she must be offered either local work, mobility to a new place of work, or retraining for a different type of work. The Board has broad powers to stimulate local private sector employment (creating private industry jobs) or to create public service jobs, for example, in road or hospital construction. If, however, there are still not enough jobs in the worker's field, he or she will be *paid* to move to a part of the country where such jobs *are* available. And, if the worker needs to be retrained for a new *type* of occupation, the Board offers a wide variety of retraining programs, which include *free* instruction, *free* teaching materials, *free* travel to the place where the training is given, tax-free allowances to help pay for rent, and tax-free funds to support workers and their families while undergoing the training. (The Board receives an open-ended appropriation from Parliament for retraining and can spend whatever is needed for this purpose.) If a retrained worker with family must move to another part of the country to start a new job, travel is paid for; financial help is given to get started in the new location; an allowance is granted for moving household goods; and, in areas where it may be hard to sell one's home, the Board may even purchase it.

All of these services are provided at the choice of the worker. No one is forced to accept any job one does not want. A worker may go through an entire retraining program, with all of its free services, and decide—without penalty—that another line of work would be better. Such a service seems to make real the statement found in the program of the ruling Swedish Social Democratic Labor Party: ''The security and self-respect which result from the knowledge that a job can always be found constitute one of the most essential conditions of human dignity in our society.''[14]

Swedes also have a myriad of public income support and other services, such as unemployment compensation, children's allowances, free education through college, housing allowances, old age pensions, cash maternity allowances at childbirth, many free medicines for expectant mothers, free housework assistance for sick or incapacitated low-income families, and even ''holidays for housewives,'' a program that provides reduced cost vacations for housewives and other women particularly in need of rest.

Swedes with whom we talked sometimes complained of high taxes to support these services, but they were quick to admit that their system has provided them with the highest living standard in Europe and has given them a deep sense of security. They have no need to fear what worries us: unemployment, irrelevant job skills, and high medical bills.

The Elderly: In Norway, we were impressed by the system of providing income security for the elderly. In the United States, older people's average income begins to drop off at age 55, then drops steeply after 65, with the result that one-sixth of the elderly live in poverty. In Norway, legislation provides for a uniform system of government pensions, usually with incomes at about two-thirds of the workers' average income during their twenty best working years. However, persons who have earned a high income during their lifetime ''will draw a lesser percentage of their peak earnings, while persons in the lowest income levels will get such a large pension, relative to their earnings, that it will amount to an old age *raise*.''[15] The theory seems to be that a more affluent person has been able to prepare better for old age, while a low-income earner needs more help to be able to live in dignity after retirement.

Housing: The most striking European experience in housing is the building of modern "new towns." Over one million people now live in the new towns in Great Britain. Most of Holland's urbanization in the coming years will be accommodated in new towns. In Sweden, Stockholm alone will soon have eighteen new towns around it.

Unlike the few new towns in the United States, none of which has substantial low or moderate income housing,[16] these European communities are built to house low-income people intermixed with others. Crowding in older cities is relieved as people move out to spacious new communities, receiving government housing subsidies, if necessary, to meet the cost of a new home or apartment. Shopping is located convenient to homes, and local industry is planned as part of the development so that jobs are available nearby for residents. Strong government controls protect the environment; parks, open space, and "green-belts" surrounding the town provide beauty and a sense of closeness to nature.

An editorial writer for the *Milwaukee Journal* reacted to a first-hand study of European cities and new towns:

After six weeks in Western Europe this spring, studying a dozen big cities, I came home convinced that it is time we watched Europe more closely—not with a sense of dread, but with a simple wish to learn. For in the way it designs new communities, combats wasteful suburban sprawl, erects decent housing for the poor, supports mass transportation in the face of fierce automobile competition, preserves charming old buildings, safeguards green space and otherwise faces the challenges of booming urbanization, the Old World often has valuable lessons for the new.[17]

In the United States: Many of these ideas and programs, of course, have been proposed, discussed, and even experimented with to a limited degree in the United States. Nearly a decade ago, Dr. Martin Luther King urged the adoption of a "Bill of Rights for the Disadvantaged," which includes ideas such as guaranteeing a good job for all those able to work and a decent living income for those who cannot work.[18] In 1966, the Freedom Budget laid out the nature and causes of poverty in the United States and the exact expenditures, timetables, and programs—in housing, health, job creation, income support, etc.—that could overcome poverty completely.[19] In 1968, the Poor People's Campaign made detailed recommendations to Congress and the Executive Branch for the elimination of poverty and racism from American life. Economists as far apart in political views as Robert Theobald and Milton Friedman have advocated a negative income tax as a means of guaranteeing to everyone in the United States a minimum income below which no one could fall.[20]

Presidential commissions, such as the National Commission on Technology, Automation and Economic Progress, have described how unemployment could be greatly reduced and millions of people put to work by expanding "public sector" jobs to meet the enormous backlog of society's public service needs.[21] It estimated that 5.3 million useful jobs could be created through public service employment in such areas as parks, streets, schools, slum areas, libraries, and hospitals.[22] The President's Commission on Income Maintenance Programs reported to President Nixon its unanimous opinion that the government should guarantee a minimum income ($2,400 for a family of four) to every American.[23] Other distinguished commissions have made recommendations in the areas of housing and health.[24]

Implications and Goals

Does all of this suggest directions for Christians concerned about economic justice? Let us look back for a moment on the ground we have covered in this chapter. We began with the biblical themes that present God as suffering with the affliction of the needy and as calling upon us to build communities of shalom. We described some of the realities of human need in this country today, and we contrasted them with programs and approaches, here and in other countries, that seem to meet the needs of the poor, at least to a large degree. It is encouraging to know that economic life can be so organized that people are *not* crushed into poverty, that the rights of the needy *are* defended, and that the desire of the afflicted *is* satisfied. (See Isaiah 3:15; Jeremiah 5:28; Isaiah 58:10.)

We can draw out from this discussion some *goals* toward which Christians should press and some general *principles* that should guide us as we try to ''seek justice, correct oppression, defend the fatherless, plead for the widow.'' (Isaiah 1:17)

• Our institutions should be designed, so far as is humanly possible, to enhance human dignity and to promote the universal common good.

• All of our citizens should go forward together. None should be left behind in poverty. People should be freed from the fear of destitution and want. All members of society should have the assurance of at least a minimum standard of living for their entire lives. Children should be able to grow up without fear of hunger; men and women should be able to live in dignity and self-respect; the elderly should look forward to their final years as a time of security and well-being.

• There should be a floor of income and services below which no one can fall. Basic services and benefits should be universally available to the entire population and should be provided either free or at a charge so low that everyone can afford them.

• Persons who are able to work should have the obligation and right to serve the community through their work, while the community has the obligation to provide useful work at decent wages.

• Weak, sick, and disabled members of society should be especially protected and helped, as should persons who have suffered due to racial or other forms of discrimination.

• The economy should not be a vehicle of sexism. Women should be freed equally with men to fulfill themselves in meaningful work and creative activity.

• The basic needs of nutritious food, meaningful work, a decent minimum income, adequate housing, good quality health care, leisure, and a secure old age should be legally guaranteed to every member of society as a matter of human right. (Perhaps we need an "Economic Bill of Rights," such as is embodied in the constitutions of some countries, to establish these rights in our own legal system.)

• These "macro"* needs require "macro" institutions to provide them. For example:

1. Institutions to guarantee to every citizen who can work either (a) meaningful work at a decent wage under decent working conditions or (b) the retraining and mobility necessary to find such work. (These guaranteed programs should be equally available to men and women and without any racial, religious, or ethnic discrimination.) Such institutions should be able to provide "public sector" jobs to help meet such public facility needs as new hospitals, schools, day care centers, and better mass transit; and such public *personnel* needs as teachers' aides, paramedical workers, visitors to the elderly to help with housework and shopping, people to help parolees coming out of prison, and recreation program developers. (Unemployed slum dwellers with manual abilities could be trained in construction and employed to build new towns for themselves, to tear down rotting slum buildings and put up new ones, to form rat and roach extermination teams, or to scrape off the lead-based paint that now kills so many of their children.) Such institutions also should be able to operate under a definition of "work" broad enough to include an education that might lead to finding a cure for cancer.

2. Mechanisms, such as the negative income tax,† to guarantee to everyone when they are unable to work, a basic minimum income, at a level in keeping with human dignity.

3. Comprehensive health services to make sure that

---

* "Macro" means "total," applying to the whole society.
† Under a negative income tax system, everyone files a Federal income tax return, but those below a poverty-level income receive payments back from the Internal Revenue Service (similar to the present refund system) to bring their income up to a minimum decent standard of living.

everyone receives the finest possible medical and dental care, regardless of ability to pay.

4. Institutions to assure decent housing for everyone, free of racial discrimination and at rental levels that all can afford.

5. Overall planning mechanisms to assure that money and services flow to where the need is, rather than just to where profit is to be made.

• The persons affected by the above programs should participate in every aspect of their development through a wide range of democratically controlled decision-making bodies, so that they can experience the realism of citizen involvement rather than the paternalism of something coming down from on high.

• Resources to meet human needs should not be drained off into war, foreign military adventures, defensive overkill, and support of foreign dictatorships.

SECTION II: ACTION FOR CHANGE

What can we do now, in practical, concrete terms to work for shalom in our economic life and in opposition to the forces that prevent its realization? We have suggested earlier that understanding and hope need to undergird Christian action and that various forms of self-education are needed to help us to grasp as deeply as possible the reality of present conditions and possible alternatives to them.

Study/Research/Education

Here are some suggestions for individual and group self-education:

Bible Study: Organize a Bible study group to read, discuss, and meditate upon the great scriptural themes of social and economic justice (e.g., Isaiah 3:14–15; Amos 5:10–24; Micah 6:6–8). What did they mean at the time they were written, and what application do they have in today's world?

Economic Justice Seminars: During 1972, a group of social change activists developed a group study method described in the pamphlet, *On Organizing Macro-Analysis Seminars* (available for 75¢ from Macro-Analysis Collective, 4719 Cedar Avenue, Philadelphia, Pa. 19143). A typical seminar meets for two or three months, one or two sessions per week, to read and discuss books and articles on economic-linked social problems, the relationship of the United States to third world countries, and the ecological challenge to traditional economic assumptions. Participants also study the political–economic systems of other nations and theories of large-scale nonviolent social change. Throughout the seminar, participants are encouraged to apply the knowledge they gain to action. Macro-Analysis seminars are now being used in adult study groups and in schools and colleges across the country.

Study Trip Overseas: Take advantage of lower group plane fares and organize a study trip to another country to see how they approach problems that perplex us. In Sweden, the Swedish Institute for Cultural Relations with Foreign Countries, an independent, nonprofit oganization, was extremely helpful in setting up contacts for us with a wide variety of people in many fields.

Living in Poverty: Try the experiment of living on a local welfare recipient's budget for a month. Ron W. Jones's book, *Finding Community,* explains how to calculate a welfare budget and how to learn from the experience of living within its limitations.[25] Such an experience may do more than many hours of reading and study to bring home the reality of poverty.

Church Services: Some years ago, I attended Sunday worship at the Central Baptist Church in Wayne, Pennsylvania. Instead of the usual service, we saw slides showing conditions of poverty and need across the United States. In the background were the recorded voices of Martin Luther King and other leaders in the struggle for justice and peace, interspersed with music from the Black Freedom movement. Members of the congregation spoke about their personal involvement in working for social justice. Our church services could experiment much more than they do with liturgies that bring home to us the relation of our faith to the oppression and affliction around us.

Dignity: This is a learning game involving four to six players. The purpose of the game is to come to understand what it is like to experience bad health, poor sanitation, prejudice, job insecurity—the plight of the poor. The playing time is 45 minutes to one and one-half hours. (*Dignity* by Kenneth Christiansen can be ordered from Friendship Press Distribution Office, P. O. Box 37844, Cincinnati, Ohio 45237.)

Jubilee: Study the Old Testament Jubilee Year, described in Leviticus 25, and organize your own modern Jubilee Festival. Use dramatization and other methods to help it come alive and to let people wrestle with its implications for today.

Action

Action based on in-depth study may be in the political area; for example: supporting legislation to guarantee adequate medical care to all citizens, fighting for programs to end hunger in America, backing measures to guarantee an adequate minimum income to everyone, a meaningful job for all who can work, and real financial security for the elderly. In voting for candidates and supporting political parties, it is important to know how they are working to shift national priorities away from military overkill and toward meeting human needs.

Many action organizations in the United States are motivated by a commitment to social justice and a desire to end destitution and oppression in our society. Many of them have local chapters and need the support and involvement of concerned people. The United Farm Workers Organizing Committee* works with farm laborers, one of the poorest and most exploited groups in our country. The National Welfare Rights Organization seeks an end to poverty and supports decent incomes and living conditions for those who cannot or should not work. The National Tenants' Organization aims to end slums and the exploi-

---

* See the Appendix for the addresses of these groups.

tative relations that often exist between landlords and tenants. The Southern Conference Educational Fund works to improve the condition of poor whites in the deep South and Appalachia. The League for Industrial Democracy educates through pamphlets and other means about social problems and the potential for extending democracy into all spheres of American life. The Southern Christian Leadership Conference uses community organization and nonviolent direct action to achieve basic rights for Blacks and other poor people. The Institute for Policy Studies is a center for creative research into American social and political problems. The New Priorities Movement seeks to redirect American resources toward the solution of pressing social problems. The Movement for a New Society works with middle-class, church-related, and other people to develop nonviolent methods of achieving basic social change. There are many other groups.

Some groups work through existing professions or other institutions to generate a deep commitment to social and economic justice. Some of these groups are: the Medical Committee for Human Rights, People's Architecture, Psychologists for Social Action, Computer People for Peace, Scientists and Engineers for Social and Political Action, Sociey for Social Responsibility in Science, and the Union of Radical Political Economists.

There are, of course, many peace groups whose purpose is to reduce the amount of military spending in the United States and to turn our energies toward the tremendous unmet needs that we have ignored for so long.

Building Alternatives

Whereas most of the above organizations work primarily to change existing laws or institutions, many people are finding satisfaction in creating better approaches and institutions *now,* without waiting for government or traditional organizations to change. Our family dentist is a young man just out of dental school who has set up an alternative dental office. It is located in a slum area, and he charges extremely low rates, strictly on the basis of ability to pay. His life-style is very simple, so that he does not need a high income. He explains all of his procedures and encourages patients to hold up a mirror while he is at work, to give them a clear idea of what he is doing and to educate them about their teeth. On the wall of his waiting room is a statement, "Your Dental Rights," explaining what patients should expect and demand of dentists in terms of adequate care.

Many cities now have "free clinics," staffed by socially concerned doctors and nurses who give their sevices free or on the basis of ability to pay. Cooperative group practice of medicine is an attempt to provide care on the basis of medical need. *The People's Handbook of Medical Care,* written by two doctors, Arthur and Stuart Frank, teaches people how to take better care of themselves and how to get the best medical care for the least cost.[26]

The People's Fund in one city is an alternative to the existing United Fund. It channels monies to organizations working for fundamental social and economic change. This approach seeks not only to serve but to change the conditions that make people need service.

Many people are starting cooperatives of various kinds —in housing, credit, and food retailing—in the belief that cooperatives are less oriented to profit and more designed to respond to people's real needs.

Nonviolent Direct Action

Nonviolent direct action is a potent method for struggling for economic justice. Christian nonviolence might be described as an effort to resist evil and to reaffirm the good in accordance with the mind of Christ. It seeks to confront and to change oppressive conditions while maintaining an attitude of good will toward those who may be perpetuating the oppression.

In modern times, Dr. Martin Luther King has been the main Christian advocate of nonviolence in America and has shown its power in building human dignity and changing unjust social conditions. One of the tragedies of Dr. King's assassination is that he was in the process of developing the Poor People's Campaign, which intended to focus the attention of the nation on the economic plight of poor people from all races and backgrounds.

It seems inevitable, nevertheless, that we will again see poor people in this country coming together (as Cesar Chavez is doing with farm workers), using nonviolent direct action as a means of changing the structures that hold them in oppression. Christians, followers of the One who came with the power of love to set at liberty those who are oppressed, are called upon to make every effort to help this come about.

Questions for Discussion

1. Do you know of countries where poverty has been eliminated? If so, how has this come about?
2. Why has the United States failed to rid itself of poverty and hunger when it is such a wealthy nation?
3. How do you define "poverty"? Why do you think that people are poor in America? What steps will be necessary to eliminate poverty from American life?
4. Should our society guarantee to every citizen the basic needs of nutritious food, meaningful work, a decent minimum income, adequate housing, good quality health care, leisure, and a secure old age? How? If not, how do we deal with poverty?

68

Suggested Readings

Adler-Karlsson, Gunnar. *Functional Socialism: A Swedish Theory for Democratic Socialization.* Stockholm: Primsa, 1967. A brief, readable description of the Swedish economy and social welfare system.

Cleary, David M. *Europe's Differing Health Plans.* Philadelphia: *Evening Bulletin* Reprint, 1970. A comparative study of the health care systems of various European countries.

Fleisher, Frederic. *The New Sweden.* New York: David McKay Co., 1967. A comprehensive overview of Swedish life.

A "Freedom Budget" for All Americans. New York: A. Philip Randolph Institute, 1966. The nature of poverty in the United States of America and a far-reaching proposal for ending it.

Harrington, Michael. *The Other America.* New York: Macmillan, 1962. The poverty described by Harrington a decade ago points out that many people in the "Other America" never got over the economic depression of the 1930s.

CHAPTER 4

Inequality:
Super-Rich and Super-Poor

SECTION I: WHAT IS AND WHAT MIGHT BE

Biblical Perspective

Discussions of economic justice are prone to focus on those who have too little, who suffer from poverty, deprivation, and oppression. But the Bible is also concerned about those who have *too much* and with a society that is polarized by inequality. It holds out a vision of a society where the wealth of one person is not based on exploitation of another and where a spirit of familyhood leads those with abundance to supply the wants of others, "that there may be equality." (2 Corinthians 8:14)

The Bible often refers to the tendency of people with preponderant wealth to use it to exploit others. In the message of the prophets is God's condemnation of the rich who take bribes to pervert justice and absorb the assets of the poor (Amos 5:11–12), and in the Gospels is the warning of Jesus to his disciples against the long-robed, well-to-do people who "devour widows' houses." (Mark 12:38–40) All of this is contrary to the biblical notion that human beings are precious in God's sight, that they are to be treated as ends and not means to someone else's enrichment, and that they are to work together in service to the common good.

The New Testament goes even further in its critique of wealth-seeking: the wealthy are viewed as being in great spiritual danger (Matthew 19:23–24; Luke 16:19–31) and the pursuit of riches is strongly reproved (Luke 12:15; Matthew 6:24). Simplicity of outward possessions and richness of inner spirit, combined with life in loving community, are the ideals.

Today's Reality

The New York Times of June 4, 1970, carried an obituary of Mrs. Horace Dodge, whose estate was estimated at over $100 million.

[Mrs. Dodge died at Rose Terrace] her Versailles-style, 75-room mansion at Grosse Point Farms. At one time she owned a 100-room mansion at Palm Beach, homes in London and Southampton, and a $2 million yacht. Her jewelry collection was estimated to be worth $6 million, not including the fabulous $1 million Catherine of Russia necklace of 389 perfectly matched pearls.[1]

According to the *Times,* her fortune was accumulated through Mr. Dodge's ownership of the Dodge motor company. When he died in 1920, Mrs. Dodge's $59 million inheritance was put into tax-free municipal bonds. "The money was said to have earned on the average of $1.5 million a year, and Mrs. Dodge never had to pay a Federal income tax."[2] The *Times* predicted "tangled court battles" among grandchildren and great-grandchildren for shares of the estate and said that seven grandchildren may receive as much as $20 million each.[3]

H. Ross Perot is a Texan whose net worth has been estimated at well over $1 billion. He gained national prominence after spending about $1 million to finance a national advertising campaign in 108 of the largest newspapers in the United States and on twenty-two television outlets supporting President Nixon's Vietnam war policy—after which he was invited to a White House reception honoring Prince Philip.[4]

Charles Englehard, of New Jersey, is a "fabled multimillionaire in precious metals," owner of three private planes, a vast assemblage of art masterpieces, and millions of dollars worth of horses. His economic power in world financial circles is so great that the gold price quoted on the New York exchange has been known simply as the "Englehard quotation."[5]

The Rockefeller family has been described as having a fortune of over $5 billion, controlling the Chase Manhattan

Bank, the world's second largest bank; the world's richest real estate development; and being heavily involved in oil, international trade, and many other fields. David Rockefeller, chairman of Chase Manhattan Bank, received in 1969 a bank dividend income of $607,500 and a salary of $264,500. This salary, which reflects a raise of $11,500, was in line with the salary raises of other top executives of top banks, despite the 1969 "profit pinch." The Bank of America, the country's largest, raised its chief by $30,000 to $208,376, and the Morgan Guaranty jumped its chairman from $254,750 to $266,250.[6]

These salaries were relatively small, however, when compared to the $812,494 paid to the chairman of the International Telephone and Telegraph Company (ITT), or the $689,000 salary paid to Henry Ford II in 1971. Chairmen of the top forty-seven United States companies averaged $346,744 in salaries in 1971, which represented pay boosts averaging over 14 percent.[7] And, of course, salaries alone do not cover the many other perquisites received by corporate executives, such as stock options, health care plans, expense accounts, executive penthouses, country club memberships, private planes and cars, and deferred compensation plans.[8]

Some Causes of Inequality: What is it about our economic system that allows this vast wealth accumulation by some while millions of others suffer from acute poverty and tens of millions live in anxiety produced by economic insecurity? I do not question Mrs. Dodge's generosity and integrity as a person (she gave her 257-foot yacht to Project HOPE), but while she was entertaining two hundred guests in her marble mansion in Palm Beach with two orchestras and a champagne fountain, children not far away were living in shacks and going hungry. While Mr. Englehard manipulates the gold market, farm workers in his state labor in the fields, and feel that they have had a good year if they earn $3,000. While Mr. Perot was giving $1 million to support President Nixon's war policy, millions of Americans did not stop worrying about how to pay their ever-increasing bill for food and medicine.

According to lawyer-economist-business consultant

Louis O. Kelso, author of *The Capitalist Manifesto,* the enormous disparity in wealth and income in the United States is due primarily to the way in which income-producing capital is owned. Kelso points out that all wealth in any society is produced by labor (the human factor in production) and capital (the nonhuman factor—land, machines, factories, etc.).[9] In our highly technological society, there has been a tremendous acceleration in the use of capital in production. Instead of doing mathematics by hand with a pen, we now use high-speed computers; instead of carrying goods on our backs or on a horse, we use fleets of trucks, trains, and planes. Capital now creates about 90 percent of our society's total wealth.

Whereas "labor power" is pretty much equally distributed among the population (everyone has one head, two arms, and two legs), the ownership of productive capital is *not* equally distributed. Over thirty million Americans own some stock, but only about 2 percent of the families in the United States own most of the productive, wealth-producing capital, primarily through ownership of corporate stocks and bonds.

This monopoly of capital ownership means that the owners also have a monopoly on the wealth that the capital produces. Because it is capital that produces the most wealth, it is the minority who owns most of the capital and who receives the preponderant income of society. People who own capital can have large incomes without working at all, while nonowners can work extremely hard (e.g., as a Mexican-American migrant farm laborer) and still live in poverty. It is no longer true that everyone has an equal chance if he or she is just willing to work. Charles Englehard and David Rockefeller do not earn their millions through energetic labor (though they may be hard workers), but through their ownership of the capital that produces society's greatest wealth.

Much of this wealth is now concentrated in large corporations, which dominate the American economy. The $24 billion revenue of General Motors, for example, is larger than the state revenues of California, New York, Pennsylvania, Illinois, Texas, and Ohio *combined.* It is larger than the gross national product of any African country or any Latin American country except Brazil. This makes the running of General Motors comparable to that of a large nation.

Economist Robert Heilbroner estimates in his book, *The Limits of American Capitalism,* that if the top 150 corporations stopped functioning for some reason, the United States would be paralyzed. Cities would starve for lack of rail and truck transportation, light and power would flicker out in major urban areas, telephone communication would cease, food and consumer goods distribution would collapse, and most American families would go bankrupt.[10]

Given this concentration of wealth and power, it is not surprising that the statistics on income and wealth in the United States show a land of marked inequality, an inequality that has remained virtually unchanged since World War II. The richest 20 percent of United States families has received more of the nation's income since World War II than the bottom 60 percent. The richest fifth receives 45 percent of all salary income and over 60 percent of all personal business and property income.[11] ("If money income had been divided equally among families in 1970, the average income for each family would have been over $11,000.")[12]

There is an even greater degree of inequality in the statistics of *wealth* (i.e., people's possessions and property, as distinct from their money income).

For instance, in 1962 the top fifth, ranked by income size, received 41.7% of personal *income*; the top fifth, ranked by wealth size, owned 77% of personal *wealth*. The total wealth of the top 20% of families was three times greater than the entire wealth of the bottom 80%. The top 1% of families and unrelated individuals receives at the most 9% of personal *income*; the top *1%* of individual wealthholders owns between *20% and 30%* of all personally held *wealth* and has done so for decades.[13]

The most significant form of wealth, of course, is the kind that also produces income for its owner, such as apartments whose ownership produces rents, and stock which produces dividends. This wealth is heavily concentrated at the top, with the top 2 percent of Americans owning about 80 percent of privately held corporate stock, 90 percent of privately held corporate bonds, and nearly 100 percent of privately held (mostly tax-free) municipal bonds.[14]

I used to think that there were income redistribution mechanisms in the United States (such as progressive taxation and government transfer payments) that reduced to some degree the holdings of the rich, both leveling disparities and channeling some funds to the needy poor. But the truth seems to be that taxes and other mechanisms are having very little effect on redistribution and that inequality is actually *growing*.

Mrs. Dodge's investment in tax-free municipal bonds is only one example of how the wealthy can sidestep the tax bite through the utilization of myriad loopholes. Do you remember the furor in April 1971, when it was discovered that fifty-six American millionaires paid *no* tax in 1970 to the Internal Revenue Service? But this is only the top of the loophole iceberg: although the Federal individual income tax is nominally progressive, ranging from 50 percent to 70 percent in the top brackets, the effective rates (the taxes actually paid) have recently been as low as 26 percent for the top 1 percent of income earners. Inheritance taxes on wealth nominally range to 77 percent, but the effective rate, it has been estimated, is less than 10 percent. The use of tax loopholes has enabled some large corporations to pay no Federal income taxes. Others have paid at a rate under 20 percent while small corporations, with fewer loophole advantages, have paid at a rate above 40 percent.[15]

The low effective rates come from the loopholes provided in the tax laws in the form of preferential treatment of capital gains, oil depletion allowances, depreciation writeoffs, and interest on state and local bonds. This means that present taxes have an extremely modest effect on income and wealth distribution, and the gap (in absolute dollars) between the rich and the poor actually *grows* each year.[16]

Some Effects of Inequality: What is the effect of this enormous inequality on other aspects of our life? A few illustrations follow.

Great wealth brings with it political influence unavailable to the less-monied citizen. On election day, we are all about equal—President, farmer, teacher, and laborer—standing in the poll booth with our one vote. But *before* the election we know how dependent the candidates are on large contributions (or their own personal wealth) to be able to spend the millions often required to carry out a campaign. (The 1968 Presidential campaign is estimated to have cost the candidates $100 million.)

This has led to what Common Cause, the citizens' lobby, has called "the forced dependence of many candidates on a few wealthy individuals and special interest groups for funds."[17] Common Cause notes that insurance executive W. Clement Stone, for example, paid out at least $500,000 (and perhaps $1 million) to Richard Nixon's 1968 presidential campaign.[18] On the Democratic side, Common Cause found that almost 25 percent of the contributions to the campaign of Senator John Sparkman (Alabama Democrat), chairman of the Senate Committee on Banking, Housing and Urban Affairs, came from individuals and groups associated with banking, housing, or building trade activities.[19]

Such a system, says Common Cause, "gives some individuals greatly disproportionate influence over public policy, and reduces the impact of the average citizen on his elected representatives." One White House aide said, "If I give $100,000 and you give $10, of course I have more pull . . . And I should. I have a bigger stake in things than you do."[20] This suggests that practices may not have changed too much from the early 1900's when Senator Boies Penrose told a group of businessmen that he believed in a division of labor: "You send us to Congress; we pass laws under . . . which you make money; . . . and out of your profits you further contribute to our campaign funds to send us back again to pass more laws to enable you to make more money."[21]

In addition to campaign contributions is the possibly even greater impact of well-financed lobbies and special-interest-funded "think-tanks" and opinion-forming groups that make their influence felt *after* elections.

The political impact of wealth is so great that some analysts have described the American political system as a plutocracy (government by the wealthy). In any case, it is clear that democracy is seriously undercut and damaged by the inequitable distribution of wealth, and that the lack of adequate spending to meet the needs of the poor and of the public sector is related to the overinfluence of wealthy people in politics.

Welfare for the Rich: Many Americans are convinced that their tax dollars are being spent to subsidize handouts to the poor, most of whom could be self-supporting if only they were willing to work. Would they feel the same if they realized that "less than 1% of the nation's welfare recipients are able-bodied men" and that the vast majority of people on welfare are elderly (24 percent), permanently and totally disabled (8 percent), blind (1 percent), children (50.3 percent), incapacitated parents in the home (2.9 percent), or mothers (13 percent)?[22]

Many Americans believe that a large portion of United States tax money is spent in welfare for the poor. The truth, however, is that less than 2 percent of the Federal budget goes for public welfare payments, and this usually provides amounts at such a low level (e.g., fifty-nine dollars per month for a Mississippi welfare mother) that most recipients *still* live below the poverty line.

What *is* startling to note, however, is the very large amount of the Federal budget that goes into a host of subsidy programs channeling tax dollars to the *affluent.* A recent study by the United States Congress's Joint Economic Committee, *The Economics of Federal Subsidy Programs,* showed that Federal government subsidies cost taxpayers more than $63 billion per year—*fifteen times* as much as the $4.2 billion allocated in the 1971 budget for welfare.[23]

A few of these subsidies (e.g., for medical research and job training) do help poor people, along with other Americans. But by far the largest part of the $63 billion is spent solely to "help" the already affluent. To give but one example:

Agricultural subsidies of $10 billion per year give the wealthiest farm families benefits averaging $14,000 apiece (raising their net farm income from $13,400 to $27,500), while the poorest 40% receive an average benefit of $300 (boosting them to a net farm income of $1,100) . . . The poorer half of the farm population receives 9.1% of the total Federal subsidy, while the wealthiest 19% takes home 62.8% of the Federal money.[24]

In 1970, subsidies such as this gave Senator James Eastland $146,000 in Federal money for not planting cotton on his Mississippi plantation. There is a plethora of other Federal subsidies—housing for the middle class and the rich, salary subsidies for shipping companies, funds to the tobacco industry, grants and loans to airlines, ammunition and guns to the National Rifle Association, and many other programs.

Is there justification for calling these expenditures "welfare for the rich"? Is it not true that the inequitable distribution of income and wealth in the United States not only undercuts political democracy and programs to help the needy but also raids the Treasury and channels a disproportionate share of public funds to those individuals and businesses who need them least?

What Are the Alternatives?

Can our economic life be organized so that there is a greater degree of equality, both in the distribution of income and wealth and in the distribution of decision-making power?

This section on alternatives to inequality in our economic life cannot be as explicit as the section on human need. Whereas there has been a great deal of thought and international experience on how to overcome poverty and to create a minimally secure economic system, there is much less solid information on how to overcome inequality. The dichotomy between super-rich and super-poor, the powerful and the relatively powerless, is certainly not unique to the United States; few nations have achieved an economy approaching an equitable distribution among citizens of income, wealth, and power. It is easy to believe that this dichotomy is the way it was meant to be.

If we wish to be open to the shalom that God intends for humanity, however, then we have an obligation to try to make equality more real in our own economic system.

China: The only large, modern society that seems to approach economic equality is China. I mention China with some apprehension, knowing the deep gulf that divides our two nations and anticipating the hostility with which some readers may greet any favorable discussion of that country. In spite of the recent thaw in United States– Chinese relations, Cold War tensions and ideological conflicts still persist. And the view of China that even sympathetic visitors are reporting shows a society of frightening conformity, restrictions on freedom, official atheism, and other features that conflict with our deepest values. When we add to all this such factors as historical and cultural disparities and different stages of economic development, it is hard to see ways that we can learn from China.

However, I believe that there is value in noting that some economic problems that we have assumed were unsolvable in fact have already been solved by others. For example, China, a land somewhat larger than the United States with a population four times as large as ours, had a colossal problem of inequality, which they have apparently gone a long way toward overcoming. John Roderick writes in *The New York Times* of the changes he noted on returning to Shanghai after twenty-five years:

It was a city of underfed rickshaw boys, filthy slums, and dying poor. Outside the Broadway mansions, where I lived for a year, the teeming sampans, crowded with the starving, made many well-fed Americans avert their faces. The extremes of wealth and poverty were appalling.

Today there are no beggars, no rickshaws, no poor dying in the streets . . . The rich and the poor are no more . . . Where once millions died of famine, everyone—at least in the areas visited—seemed to have enough to eat. The ordinary people appeared sturdy, healthy, and content.[25]

A 1972 Quaker delegation to China (some members of whom had done medical work there in the 1940's) commented:

The luxury-loving officials, landlords, and merchants of fifty or twenty-five years ago, with their often ostentatious lifestyles, are gone, as are the starving, ragged, diseased peasants or urban poor, who were far more numerous. Greed on the part of an affluent few and grinding poverty on the part of the many were responsible for growing corruption, theft, and violence before 1949 . . . Corruption and theft [now] are virtually unknown; people are probably safer in their persons and possessions in 1972 than most other places in the world, even on unlit city streets and alleyways at night. In the 1940's one had constantly to guard against theft; in 1972 . . . we had difficulty getting rid of unwanted things even by putting them in waste baskets—conscientious hotel staff or our Chinese travel guides would keep returning them to us.[26]

Facts such as these led *Fortune* magazine editor and visitor to China Louis Kraar to write of the "pervasive egalitarianism" that characterizes modern China.[27] And it is facts such as these that may help us to put aside ideological differences and look at some of the practices that China has adopted to bring about and to maintain this transformation. For example:

1. Setting salaries on an industry-wide basis so that differentials rarely are larger than one to ten. (The United States differential is more like one to 200 or more, i.e., from a minimum wage income of $4,000 to the ITT chairman's salary of $800,000 plus.)

2. Setting prices so that there is little or no inflation and at a level low enough so "that essentials such as food, clothing, housing and medical care are accessible

to all.''[28] Return visitors to China are surprised to find prices of meat and other products exactly the same over a ten-year period. Rent ranges from 2 percent to 5 percent of income and clothes and furniture are inexpensive.

3. Providing free or minimal cost services and income support, such as extensive medical care for the whole population and retirement pensions at 70 percent of pay.

4. Eliminating all personal income tax and providing public services out of the earnings of agriculture and industry.

5. Protecting private ownership of houses, personal belongings, and small plots of land (for growing things such as pigs, chickens, and vegetables), but bringing under social ownership all productive capital, such as shops, industries, and large agricultural lands, so that no one will gain inordinate wealth through ''property income.'' (Heavy industry may be state-owned, while agricultural areas may be owned collectively by the peasants who work them.)

6. Eliminating former legal discrimination against women, supporting working mothers with day care and other services, and encouraging women's equal participation in work formerly considered the province of men. (Almost one-third of Chinese doctors, for example, are now women.)

7. Encouraging what the *Fortune* magazine article calls participatory management, giving workers a strong decision-making voice in factory and commune, to prevent the development of a technocratic management elite.

8. Requiring professionals to do regular manual work in field and factory, so as not to become out of touch psychologically with the needs of the majority of the people. Factory administrators and engineers must work on the shop floor for a stipulated time each week or so. A hospital administrator may be required to work several days each month in janitorial duties, under the supervision of the head janitor. Students must spend time in factories or in agricultural work before going on to the university.

9. Attempting to make the spirit of *"serve the people"* a motivating force in all activity rather than the search for individual accumulation of wealth.

Of course, the insights we can gain from a society so different from the United States are limited. What we can learn is that economic problems are made by people and can be solved by people. We are not condemned by gods, fate, or invisible hands to having poverty and inequality always with us. China is one case in point. The Israeli kibbutz is another.

Israeli Kibbutzim: A high degree of equality also has been achieved in the far smaller world of the Israeli kibbutz, which is more Western than China and which provides a much higher degree of the kind of intellectual freedom to which we are accustomed. Most kibbutzim maintain complete equality in the distribution of services and income and hold all but personal property in common. Such goods and services as food, education, medical care, child care, cultural activities, and retirement are paid for out of the common funds of the kibbutz and are equally available to all members. Everyone's money income is exactly the same, regardless of the type of work performed. Lacking the monetary incentives with which we are familiar, kibbutzim are still highly productive (they comprise only about 4 percent of Israel's population, but generate 6 percent of the nation's industrial production and 33 percent of its farm production) and provide their members with a satisfying standard of living.[29]

Both China and the kibbutzim place heavy stress on service to the common good as the primary incentive for productive work. The kibbutznik's reward for hard work is not higher pay, but the respect and esteem of fellow kibbutz members, plus a sense of personal accomplishment and a contribution to the good of the whole. The Chinese worker may gain a slightly better income by accumulating "work points" or by taking on greater responsibility; but the salary range is very narrow, and there is little opportunity for personal material accumulation beyond what others also have. Western visitors report an amazing degree of internalization of Mao's slogan, "serve the people," and it seems that the drive for private aggrandizement largely has been replaced, at least for the present, by a spirit of self-sacrifice for the common welfare.

This phenomenon is reminiscent of the Gospel story of the man who asked both of his sons to work in the vineyard. One rudely refused, but later went; the other politely agreed, but failed to go. (Matthew 21:28–31) The New Testament message seems clear about what should motivate Christians in their daily life: "Let no one seek his own good, but the good of his neighbor" (1 Corinthians 10:24), "Through love be servants of one another." (Galatians 5:13) It is possible that atheistic China and Jewish Israel have gone farther toward the actual embodiment of these principles in economic life than those of us in supposedly Christian countries, where the search for personal gain and business profit are such overriding motivations. Perhaps we are saying "Yes" to the gospel of service, but doing the opposite, while other nations are saying "No" to Christianity, but trying to make service the basis of economic motivation.

Yugoslavia: A somewhat different approach to equality is seen in the Yugoslav concept of worker and community self-management. After World War II, the Yugoslavs dismantled their former system of capitalistic ownership and control of the economy. They enthusiastically adopted a Russian model of state ownership and centralized planning, only to find that, as a Yugoslav social scientist once told me, "a socialist boss can be just as bad as a capitalist boss." Workers made gains in social security and health benefits, but found that they still had little control over their lives and were being told what to do by managers appointed from above by government bureaucrats in the ministries running the economy.

A number of factors combined to make them break away from their tight alliance with the Soviet Union, and in the process they instituted their now-famous system of social ownership and worker control of the economy. Under this system, the workers of a particular enterprise are those who control its management. All workers vote regularly, by secret ballot, to elect worker candidates to a one-year term on a "workers' council," which serves as the top management body. The council sets all policy for the enterprise. Through its elected management board, it hires and fires an overall manager, decides on production, sets wage levels, borrows money, handles reinvestment, and does everything else necessary to the firm's functioning. The council also convenes all-worker meetings and organizes referenda on important issues, so that every worker has a chance to make his or her voice heard in decision-making. The local community and the national government also exercise some control, but responsibility for most decisions rests with the workers.

Yugoslavia has had many problems, including some of inequality between enterprises and between different regions of the country. However, the self-management system encourages equality in two ways: (1) It spreads wealth by making every worker a recipient of the earnings of business firms, rather than funneling profits to a capital-owning minority of the population. (2) It spreads power, by putting important decision-making ability into the hands of every worker, rather than concentrating such power in the state or in a private ownership group.

The Yugoslav system is particularly interesting in light of the 1972 study of the United States Department of Health, Education and Welfare, *Work in America,* which finds the American work force becoming more and more discontented and dehumanized and increasingly involved in drug abuse, alcohol addiction, and aggression. The report recommends, among other things, that workers be allowed to participate in business decision-making and to share in company profits.[30]

Let me stress again that there are many differences between the United States on the one hand, and China, Israel, and Yugoslavia on the other. However, from the point of view of equality, the experience of these countries suggests that an adequate approach must focus both on changing the economic structures, which inequitably distribute wealth, income, services, and power; and the economic motivations, which lead people to work primarily for their own narrow self-interest.

The United States: Americans have not been lax in proposing ways to overcome the nation's economic inequality. Much thinking has focused on our tax system, taking as given the present pattern of private ownership and profit motivation, and assuming that the way to attack inequality is through truly progressive, equitable taxation. And, indeed, inequities in taxation are a potent source of economic injustice. As Stewart Alsop pointed out in 1970:

[A rich person] can enjoy an income of $18,000 on $300,000 of capital, without paying a cent of income tax or even filing a return. A man, with a wife and two children to support, who earned that much with his brains or his muscles, would have to pay the government $3,200, if he did not want to go to jail.[31]

Other analysts have stressed how the low effective rate of gift and inheritance taxes gives radically unequal wealth to people solely because of the accident of birth. People are given a highly unequal start in life, not because of proven ability, special moral worth, or extraordinary contribution to society, but simply because of the chance happening of being born to certain parents. It is no accident that a recent Louis Harris poll showed that two-thirds of United States voters believe that "the tax laws are written for the rich and not for the average man."[32]

Suggestions for tax reform center around such issues as treating gifts and inheritances more equitably; increasing the progression of income taxes (recently cut back for high income earners); ending preferential treatment of capital gains; phasing out oil and other mineral depletion allowances; closing expense account loopholes; ending special treatment given to income made in real estate speculation; subjecting interest on state and local bonds to regular income tax; substituting progressive income taxes for regressive sales, property and flat wage taxes; making corporations (whose taxes have been cut considerably over the past two decades) pay their fair share; reducing taxes levied on work and increasing taxes on "unearned income," such as rents, interest, dividends, and inheritance.

Tax reform no doubt is desperately needed in the United States, but some American thinkers question whether we will get at the roots of inequality if we focus only on changes in the tax structure. After all, taxes have to do with levies on income *after* it has accrued to individuals and groups. A prior question is: How did the income *get to* people in such unequal portions in the first place?

To answer this question, Louis O. Kelso's description of how productive capital is owned is helpful. If most wealth is produced by capital, then there are bound to be large inequalities in wealth if only a *few* people in a society own and receive income from its productive capital. Kelso's thought-provoking solution to this dilemma is to make everyone in the United States an owner of significant portions of capital. Under his "universal capitalism" plan, there would no longer be a division between the super-rich (gaining fortunes from capital ownership) and the majority of the people (receiving most of their income from their labor alone). Rather, all would own capital, and all would enjoy the wealth it produces.[33] Kelso's plan is problematic in that it would give little real power to workers, would leave acquisitive economic motives unchanged, would require that the United States burn up an even larger share of the world's resources, and would probably exacerbate the ecological problems associated with massive economic growth.

Other economists believe that various forms of public, community, or social ownership of productive capital would be a better means of resolving the dilemma. Harvard economist John Kenneth Galbraith, for example, advocated public ownership of corporations in a recent speech before the Corporate Accountability Research Group.[34] The community ownership model is already embodied in the so-called Community Development Corporation (CDC), a community-controlled type of enterprise now operating in many parts of the United States. A CDC is owned by residents of the community in which it operates and is controlled by community people who vote (one person, one vote) on policy at membership meetings. Profits are not siphoned off to absentee owners, but are returned to the community, which may use them for improvement programs such as parks and day-care centers. (Information on CDC's may be obtained by writing the Center for Community Economic Development, 1878 Massachusetts Avenue, Cambridge, Mass. 02140.)

The *customer* ownership and control model is carried on every day in the 38,500 cooperatives that dot the American landscape. These businesses belong to the customers who use them and are democratically controlled on a "one person, one vote" basis. They engage in marketing of farm products (farm cooperatives do $19 billion worth of business per year), retail selling, and service of such needs as credit, health care, nursery schooling, and funerals The Farm Credit System, for example, has over $17 billion in loans outstanding to the one million farmers who own and control the system.

There seems to be little doubt that a fundamental approach to creating greater equality in the distribution of income and wealth must deal with the question of equitable distribution of capital ownership as well as with equalization through such measures as taxation. On the question of equitable distribution of decision-making power, it is instructive to note that Robert A. Dahl, Sterling Professor of Political Science at Yale and former president of the American Political Science Association, has argued persuasively for an industrial self-management system modeled directly on the Yugoslav experience of social ownership and worker control.[35]

Christian faith and much historical experience also suggest that inequality will not be overcome until we stop seeking individualistically for greater personal material accumulation and begin to work for the common good. As long as we are motivated to get all that we can for ourselves, our families, and the business firms with which we are associated, our economy will have a built-in tendency toward inequality.

Implications and Goals

What social implications can we draw from this for people concerned about the problem of inequality? Can we agree with the following?

• There should be a narrow spread of income and wealth, with individuals living neither in destitution nor in opulence. The economy should encourage an equitable distribution of income, wealth, services, and decision-making power.

- The economy should be ordered to give highest priority and value to human life and human well-being, rather than to money or possessions.
- People should be treated as ends, not means. Given that humans are made in the image of God, there should be respect for the dignity, capacity, and potential contribution of everyone.
- Power should be broadly distributed. People should have a right to participate in decisions affecting them, either directly or through a system of democratic representation. As much as possible, power should be localized at the community level where ordinary people can participate meaningfully in decision-making.
- Political life should be determined by democratic practices rather than by the influence of wealth. Political power should be widespread among all the people, rather than concentrated among those with preponderant wealth.
- Democratic participation in decision-making should be a reality in the economic sphere as well as in political life. The economy should be of, by, and for the people. The wealth and resources of the country should be controlled by the people (either directly or through elected representatives), rather than by a political or economic elite.
- Taxes should be designed to reduce inequality, rather than furthering it. They should be truly progressive, minimizing hardship on those with low incomes and correcting the maldistribution of income and wealth. The tax system should not discriminate against income from work by giving special privilege to unearned income (e.g., from inheritance, real estate speculation, etc.).[36] Gift and inheritance taxes should prevent the passing of large fortunes from the wealthy to their heirs. Tax loopholes and subsidies to well-heeled special interest groups and to the already wealthy should be ended.
- Prices and wages should be at a level where the lowest income earner can obtain adequate food, clothing,

shelter, medical care, and other essentials needed for a dignified life.

• Capital should be owned in such a way that the income it produces is equally available to the whole citizenry. Society's wealth should benefit all and not be appropriated by a privileged minority. There should be no nonproducing group who can live off the work of others, except for those who cannot work (children, the sick, and the disabled).

• People should be encouraged to work for the common good out of a motive of service and concern for the welfare of all, rather than in a spirit of competition for maximum personal financial gain. The spirit and institutional structure of the economy should counter such attitudes as greed, selfishness, and materialistic accumulation, and should encourage attitudes of service, cooperation, and mutual aid.

SECTION II: ACTION FOR CHANGE

Study/Research/Education

There does not seem to be one clear, resounding answer on how to bring about a society more in accord with the biblical ideal of equality. An area that does seem highly productive of inequality, however, is the American tax system, the inequities of which we have considered above. Taxation is an area of almost fantastic complexity, usually left to well-paid lobbyists and tax attorneys. But we cannot be cowed by these complexities into ignoring tax questions, for to do so hands taxation over to those who use its complexities to store up treasures on earth for themselves at the expense of those who have to carry an even heavier tax burden.

We need to study the tax system, to decide what reforms will end its inequities, and to educate ourselves and others to work for such reforms. One model for study might be a "workshop on tax loopholes," in which each member would do reading on a particular loophole and report his or her findings to the whole group, with recommendations for action.

However, as we have also stressed, inequality stems not only (and perhaps not primarily) from an inequitable tax structure but also from an inequitable distribution in the ownership and control of productive capital and from incentives based on personal and corporate income maximization. Only the most searching kind of study can show us whether a greater degree of equality can be achieved *within* the present system of ownership, control, and motivation, or whether we need to begin to work for a different kind of system. Study groups, such as the economic justice seminars mentioned in the last chapter, are one way of engaging in this deeper study.

Action

Our political action and our work with organizations will be shaped, of necessity, by the conclusions reached in our study. We will want to support those candidates, political parties, social movements, and pieces of legislation that seem to have the best hope of ending inequities.

Having engaged in some initial study, here are some areas of concern that merit particular attention as beginning steps:

1. Media campaigns and other efforts at education to bring to public attention existing inequities in wealth, income, and power, and to show the advantages to the whole society of their more equitable distribution.

2. Steps to end such injustices in the tax system as regressive taxation, which harms the poor, and tax subsidies and loopholes, which benefit only the wealthy.

3. Serious consideration of more radical steps in taxation: a negative income tax to provide a guaranteed minimum income, and taxes to establish a maximum allowable income ceiling and a maximum allowable inheritance to prevent the unjust accumulation and passing on of great riches.

4. Steps to decentralize and share power now concentrated in government bureaucracy and large corporations by bringing power more under democratic local control.

5. Measures to extend economic democracy and to

encourage a much greater degree of worker and community participation in business decision-making.

Building Alternatives

The results of study for some people may be the decision that new economic forms will be required if there is to be real impact on inequality. Such a conclusion would not be surprising, given the biblical emphasis on God's ownership and human trusteeship of the earth. As theologian Nels Ferré has written:

The Christian stewardship of property starts with the assertion that under God we have all things in common. No one lives unto himself alone and no one has property unto himself alone. Each one lives as a fellowship member and each one has property as a fellowship member.[37]

It may be that Christians will pioneer in conceiving of and bringing about new ways of owning and controlling property that will be more in harmony with the primitive church's concept of its common ownership and use for the common good. Perhaps new economic forms will be discussed that do not require a primary emphasis on profit maximization, but that encourage people to act out of a concern for mutual well-being. And Christians should certainly be at the forefront of any movement to replace greed and self-seeking with motives of love and service, which were so emphasized by Jesus and the apostles.

Given such possibilities, one practical step is to begin now to study, build, and experiment with new economic forms. Some efforts in this direction are already in motion. Of particular interest is the "Exploratory Project for Economic Alternatives,"* a sophisticated undertaking by economists, researchers, and others who are interested in forms of ownership and control that are neither capitalism nor bureaucratic socialism. They are looking into the equality-creating potential of such economic forms as community development corporations, cooperatives, local

---

* See appendix for address.

public ownership of new towns, employee trusts, land trusts, and municipally owned utilities. They hope both to support such alternatives and to bring to public attention a concrete description of how the American economy might be more equitably organized. I recently talked with a deeply committed Christian from Wichita, Kansas, who is working to convert his printing business from one that *he* owns and manages to one that will be owned and controlled by all the workers in the plant. The Yugoslav concept of social ownership and worker self-management was of great interest to him.

At a different level, some New Englanders are planning to set up a new town, based on democratic decision-making in economic as well as political affairs, community ownership of land and productive property, and an equitable distribution of income and wealth. Through their New Town Project they hope to create a concrete, visible alternative from which people can learn.

A more agriculturally oriented new town has been set up in southwest Georgia by a group called "New Communities, Inc.," with the help of national church groups. It is based on the ownership idea of a "land trust."

On a smaller but still significant level, organizing and operating a cooperative is a way to gain experience with a form of ownership and control different from that usually practiced in our economy. A clear description of how to start a cooperative store, for example, is found in Ron W. Jones's book, *Finding Community*.[38] (The Cooperative League of the U.S.A. is an excellent source of many free books, films, and pamphlets on the cooperative movement.)

Questions for Discussion

1. How can people best work for greater economic equality?
2. Do you believe that our tax system has favored the wealthy? If so, why?
3. What features of our economic system produce the large gap between the very rich and the very poor?
4. Is some degree of economic inequality good, for example, as a spur to effort and achievement?
5. What is ownership? Why own something? If ownership is for the common good, why not have common ownership?
6. To what extent do we have "economic democracy" in the United States? Is this something that should be extended? If so, how?
7. What are the alternative forms of reward and incentive besides the acquisition of wealth?
8. What would you include in an economic bill of rights?

Suggested Readings

Domhoff, G. William. *The Higher Circles*. New York: Random House, 1970. The political power of Americans of great wealth.

Green, Mark J., Fallows, James M., and Zwick, David R. *Who Runs Congress?* New York: Bantam Books, 1972. The inordinate influence of wealth and lobbies on Congress.

Harrington, Michael. *Why We Need Socialism in America*. New York: Norman Thomas Fund, 1970. The author argues that basic problems can only be solved through a socialist political economy.

Keyserling, Leon H. *Taxation of Whom and For What?* Washington, D.C.: Conference on Economic Progress, 1969. Basic questions about inequities in our tax system.

Kolko, Gabriel. *Wealth and Power in America.* New York: Frederick A. Praeger, 1962. The structural causes of poverty in America.

Lundberg, Ferdinand. *The Rich and the Super-Rich.* New York: Lyle Stuart, 1968. A monumental study of America's richest families.

Stern, Philip. *The Rape of the Taxpayer.* New York: Random House, 1973. Loopholes allow the wealthy to escape their share of taxes, while the rest of us pay more.

Upton, Letitia, and Lyons, Nancy. *Basic Facts: Distribution of Personal Income and Wealth in the United States.* Cambridge: Cambridge Institute booklets, May, 1972. A clear, brief study of maldistribution of wealth in the United States.

CHAPTER 5

A Family Riding on Spaceship Earth

SECTION I: WHAT IS AND WHAT MIGHT BE

Biblical Perspective

The Bible pictures a God who wants us to live in the world as members of a human family and with an attitude of stewardship toward the world of nature, the precious, intricate, beautiful earth that he has lovingly placed in our care. The earth is the Lord's, full of the teeming life that he created (Psalm 24:1), but he shares his dominion with human beings, asking us to tend and care for it according to his will and as trustees for him.

The resources of the planet are to be used to help create a world of shalom, which means not only peace, but well-being, wholeness, justice, and community. The afflicted and oppressed in any nation are deprived of their rightful shalom, and God stands with them (Psalm 103:6; Luke 1:52–53), calling on his children to combat the forces arrayed against shalom. He loves justice and hates it when humans rob and exploit one another (Isaiah 61:8).

Injustice, greed, and covetousness are forces that break shalom, disrupting not only humans' relation with one another, but their relation with the natural world. Shalom comes by following God's way. I believe this includes sharing possessions (Luke 3:11) and living a simple life, while rejecting covetousness and storing up treasures for oneself. In Jesus' teaching, the "rich" are those of few possessions (Luke 12:15, 33), and it is the gentle who are rightful inheritors of the earth (Matthew 5:5).

In modern terminology, this vision of a world community traveling through the solar system has been described as a spaceship—"the spaceship earth."

Today's Reality

The Broken Human Family: During the summer of 1971, many people became aware of a terrible tragedy in Pakistan. National magazines carried stories of massacres of thousands of unarmed civilians by government soldiers and the flight of millions of starving, terrorized refugees into India. General Yahya Khan, military dictator of Pakistan, precipitated the tragedy by sending 60,000 troops into what was then East Pakistan. His purpose was to crush a political movement that had just won a democratic election by an overwhelming majority and that apparently threatened his dictatorial power.

Some of us in the Movement for a New Society had organized an economic justice seminar to study the impact of United States government and business practices on other nations. Knowing almost nothing about Pakistan, we were surprised to learn that the United States had equipped Pakistan's army with $1 billion worth of military aid and, since 1954, had supplied more than $4 billion of economic assistance, about one-half of Pakistan's foreign aid total. (*Newsweek* reported that twenty-two Pakistani families, helped by such funds, gained ownership or control of "66% of Pakistan's industry, some 80% of its banking and insurance assets and vast tracts of the country's best farmland." This super-rich group built up huge foreign holdings in Swiss and other banks that one source estimated at "as much as half a billion dollars . . . more than twice Pakistan's foreign currency reserves."[1])

Reacting in horror to the brutality of military suppression, other Western nations cut off aid at the recommendation of the World Bank. Our own government (at first covertly and then openly) continued its shipments. American economic aid was thus used to undergird General Khan's strained economy, and United States Sabre jets, tanks, and guns were used to crush the results of a democratic election.

Sometimes one needs to do extraordinary things to bring extraordinary changes. Believing in the efficacy of nonviolent direct action and wanting to protest our government's involvement, the Movement for a New Society organized a "nonviolent fleet" of canoes and kyacks and attempted to block Pakistani ships when they sailed into the ports of Baltimore, New York, and Philadelphia. The mass media took an interest in this "nonviolent blockade." We received crucial help from the International Longshoremen's Association (ILA). The president of one ILA local stated that loading Pakistani ships would be the same as assisting in genocide.

Working with the longshoremen, we closed the port of Philadelphia to Pakistani ships and generated worldwide publicity about United States involvement in General Khan's pogrom. We also worked closely with members of Congress who finally got the United States to suspend aid to Pakistan, and we took deep satisfaction in making some small contribution to freeing the people of Bangladesh from an oppressive dictatorship.*

Subsidized Oppression: An experience such as this is bound to raise questions in one's mind about the relation of the United States to *other* nations around the world. Is our support for the Pakistani dictatorship an unfortunate, unique aberration? Does the weight of our influence tend to fall on behalf of such systems of oppression and domination or on the side of the forces making for shalom?

Our relations with other nations, especially in the so-called third world, are all too similar to our involvement in Pakistan. And there seems to be a disturbing link between our economic needs and our relationship to dictatorships around the world.

- In 1973, the United States will provide over $9.5 billion in military assistance to foreign countries and only $3.7 billion in economic and humanitarian aid. (Before 1946, the United States gave no foreign military assistance in peacetime.) We have over half a million military personnel overseas at 192 major and 1,221 minor military installations. Twenty-five of the sixty-four nations who will receive United States military assistance in 1973 "are governed by the military or permit no open opposition to the government."[2]

---

* This story is told in more detail in an article, "Blockading for Bangladesh," *Progressive 36* (February 1972): 20.

- The United States spends millions of dollars every year to assist and train the police forces of repressive governments around the world.[3] Perhaps the most shocking instance is the twelve-year-long United States training program for over 100,000 Brazilian police. Brazil, a military dictatorship, has received worldwide criticism for its brutal suppression of political opposition and for police torture of political prisoners, including priests and nuns. Pope Paul said of Brazil: "The church will no longer tolerate the commission of atrocities and tortures in a country that calls itself Christian."[4] A police chief and his assistant were excommunicated after stripping a Roman Catholic nun naked and applying electric shocks to her sex organs.

In spite of this, the United States has poured economic and military aid into Brazil, and maintains our largest Latin American military mission there. When the ruling generals made their coup in 1964, Lincoln Gordon, the United States ambassador, hailed it as being "as significant to the defense of the Free World as the Sino-Soviet split and the success of the Marshall Plan."[5] President Johnson sent "warm wishes."[6]

Brazil is known for its eagerness to bring in foreign private investment. It is estimated that over 80 percent of Brazil's manufacturing industry is owned by foreigners, mostly Americans. One-fifth of our South American investments are in Brazil, and many large American corporations operate there. Brazil's gross national product has soared, but most benefits go to the top income group. Eighty percent of the people live below an income of $350 per year.[7] Brazil's Finance Minister has admitted that only 5 percent of the country's people have benefited from economic growth, that "45% actually had their standard of living eroded, and the rest live as they did before the boom started."[8]

- The United States maintains a close alliance with Portugal, giving a great deal of financial aid, including $436.5 million in credits in 1972. Portugal is one of the last nations to keep colonies in Africa. Their troops (some of them trained in the United States) use napalm and bombing of civilians to try to suppress local freedom movements. United States corporations, most notably Gulf Oil, have large investments in Portuguese colonies.

• The duly-elected government of Guatemala threatened in the early 1950s to divide up United Fruit Company's vast holdings. Later it was revealed that President Eisenhower used the Central Intelligence Agency (CIA) to overthrow the government.[9] According to Gunnar Myrdal, United Fruit now controls "the entire economic life of six Latin American countries."[10] A similar CIA action overthrew the Iranian government of Mossadeq, who had threatened Western oil interests, and installed a new premier who concluded an agreement highly favorable to United States oil companies.[11] More recently the ITT conglomerate tried to arrange similar CIA pressure against the democratically elected government of Salvador Allende in Chile. Senator Everett Dirksen of Illinois listed in the *Congressional Record* in 1969, 162 United States military interventions (all of them unauthorized by Congress) in foreign countries from 1795 to 1945 "to protect U.S. interests."[12]

• President Nixon recently stated that only thirty of the ninety-one countries to whom we give military or economic aid "have leaders who are there by any standard that we would consider fair."[13]

• According to one study, the United States has opposed virtually all the developing nations' recent proposals to overcome inequities in the international economic system.[14] This country has supported a trade system that pays low prices to poor nations for their raw materials, while charging them high prices for our manufactured goods. This has contributed to the growing gap between rich and poor nations, to a world in which a half billion people are starving or chronically hungry, while the United States—6 percent of the world's population—accounts for some 40 percent of the world's annual consumption. As Brazilian Catholic Bishop Helder Camara has put it: "Today 85%, tomorrow 90% [in the underdeveloped world] rot in misery in order to make possible the excessive comfort of 15%, tomorrow 10%, of the world's population."[15]

• The United States is now dependent on other nations

for needed resources. We have shifted from a net exporter to a net importer of metals and minerals. Many of these imports come from the subsidiaries of United States corporations that operate in underdeveloped nations, extracting the resources and shipping them to the United States. Investment by private United States companies in poor nations is expanding. About 20 percent of United States corporate profits come from foreign investments, with two-thirds of these profits coming from the third world. In 1970, "the rate of return on investments in less developed countries was 21 percent, roughly twice the yield on investments in the developed areas."[16] And, as Senator Charles Mathias, Jr., of Maryland has pointed out, the capital flow from an area such as Latin America into the United States is "now over four times as great as the flow south."[17] This means that poor nations are, in a sense, giving foreign aid to the United States!

• United States corporations, according to Senator Frank Church of Idaho, first decapitalize Latin America, then plow back some of their profits "to gain increasing control of the mineral assets, industry, and production of Latin American countries."[18] The result is that much of the economic life of Latin America is now dominated by United States businesses, which "control or decisively influence between 70 and 90 percent of the raw material resources of Latin America, and probably much more than half of its modern manufacturing industry, banking, commerce and foreign trade, as well as much of its public utilities."[19] Because these companies are interested in a stable climate for investment, they find it easy to link up with local oligarchies and strong-arm governments, which favor such investment and which suppress popular movements threatening foreign corporations.[20] And, because the United States government is so heavily influenced by the business point of view, it is all too ready to use military or other pressure to support United States overseas businesses and the dictatorial regimes with which they are often allied.

The Exploited Earth: If our relation with other world nations seems often to fall on the side of domination and oppression, what about our relation to the world of nature —the ecosystem on whose intricate balances all life depends? Our ecological awareness is probably higher than at any time in human history, and we only need touch upon the sobering facts that the ecologists have been hammering home.

We know that Lake Erie is "dead," killed by industrial wastes that make no life in it possible except for slime, sludge worms, and a poison-imbibing mutant of carp. But we also know that Lake Erie is only one example of thousands of lakes and rivers (in socialist as well as capitalist countries) that are being killed by pollution. And we are more aware than ever of the fact that the earth's waters do not have an infinite capacity to absorb effluents, that the day can easily come when they will no longer "bring forth swarms of living creatures" (Genesis 1:20), but will instead become a source of death. Already, people who bathe on certain polluted European beaches are twice as susceptible to infection as those who do not.

We have heard that industries in Venice, where air pollution is eroding priceless monuments, have been ordered to supply their 50,000 workers with gas masks.[21] We have read that a five-day bout of air pollution killed 4,000 Londoners in 1952. But, beyond this, we know that the world's thin film of life-giving air cannot forever sustain the assault of pollution from our smokestacks and exhaust pipes. In 1968, a UNESCO conference predicted that the planet would start to become uninhabitable in about twenty years because of air pollution alone.[22]

The same kinds of grim facts could be cited concerning soil pollution, the ever-increasing depletion of non-renewable mineral resources, the population explosion, the limits of world food supply, and other aspects of the ecological crisis. It is these facts that moved thirty-three of the United Kingdom's most distinguished scientists to endorse in 1972 a "Blueprint for Survival," in which they predict that unrestricted industrial and population expansion, with its attendant pollution and exhaustion of resources, will lead to "the breakdown of society and of the life support systems on this planet—possibly by the end of this century and certainly within the lifetime of our children."[23]

Indeed, it is a sense of the fragility of the earth and of the limits of its ability to accommodate a growth-oriented humankind which is forcing itself on human consciousness. Infinite growth, we are realizing, cannot be sustained in a world of finite resources and finite pollution-absorbing capacity. "Spaceship earth" cannot forever keep taking on more passengers, burning more and more of its skin for fuel, and pumping more and more pollutants into its air system.

High-consumption, industrialized societies such as the United States are especially resource-damaging and pollution-causing. One prominent scientist estimates that the world could sustain a population of only 500 million (nowhere near its present 3.5 billion, much less the 7 billion expected just after the year 2000) living according to American standards.[24] Each American uses about twenty times as much of world energy resources (coal, gas, etc.) as the average citizen of China and "has roughly fifty times the negative impact on the Earth's life-support systems as the average citizen of India."[25]

Yet all United States projections are for even higher rates of resource use—for example, a doubling of our need for electricity every ten years for the foreseeable future. It would seem our industrial system is oriented around the very economic growth that distinguished scientists are telling us the world cannot long sustain.

Antispaceship Economics: Why is it that we so disregard the fragile ecosystem and treat with such harshness so many of our family members around the world? Mohandas Gandhi once said that the world has enough for everybody's need, but not for everybody's greed. Have we not built our economic system largely on the principle of greed—on the Adam Smith idea that each person's pursuit of his or her own self-interest will somehow lead to the social good? Have we not taught our people (and anyone else who comes within range of our advertising) that, contrary to Jesus' teaching in Luke 12:15, covetousness is a *good* thing and a person's life *does* consist in the abundance of his or her possessions? Have we not based our total economic system on the dynamics of maximum consumption, maximum growth, maximum profit?

If the answer to these questions is even a partial "yes," then it is not surprising that we find our corporations spread over the world, allying themselves with any system that will give access to the resources we need for our consumption. It is not surprising, as ecologist Barry Commoner points out in his fascinating book, *The Closing Circle*,[26] that our industry creates the technologies and the products that bring the most profit, even though these are usually the very items (synthetics, plastics, high powered cars, detergents, and chemical fertilizers) that are most damaging to the environment.

What Are the Alternatives?

If we ever are to live in harmony with the ecosystem and the rest of the human family, it seems clear that we will have to achieve basic, unprecedented changes in our economic system. Economists, ecologists, and others are beginning to construct models that fit the ecological-planetary imperative. The "Suggested Readings" at the end of this chapter list a number of books and articles that include creative attempts at such model-building.

These thinkers face an immense task, because their work necessarily challenges many of the basic assumptions that have undergirded economic thought for two centuries. They realize that neither socialist nor capitalist societies have many answers to their questions. Rather than positing a "frontier" or "cowboy" economy, with unlimited resources and unlimited space to throw away waste, they work within the framework of a "spaceship" economy. Rather than assuming that all growth in gross national product is good, they question the desirability of growth and seek only those forms of expansion that do the least damage to the ecosystem. Rather than accepting waste and obsolescence, they opt for long-term durability of products. They focus on the moral imperative of more equitable distribution of existing income and wealth, rather than on the improved expectation that increased societal

104

wealth will "trickle down" to benefit the poor. They recommend recycling, frugality, simplicity, and planning, instead of junking, high consumption, profit-seeking, and a free market.

Christians working as scientists and concerned citizens undoubtedly will be involved in the search for an ecologically sound, nonexploitative alternative, but is it not true that Christian faith itself has a potentially profound contribution to make? Arnold Toynbee has written that our problem, at bottom, is spiritual.

We are suffering from having sold our souls to the pursuit of an objective that is both spiritually wrong and practically unattainable. We have to reconsider our objective and to change it. Unless and until we do this, we shall not have peace either among ourselves or within each of us.[27]

Christians have lived more or less comfortably with a wealth-oriented economic system ever since industrialization took root in Western culture. Contrast this orientation, however, with a biblical statement such as the following:

We brought nothing into the world, and we cannot take anything out of the world; but if we have food and clothing, with these we shall be content. But those who desire to be rich fall into temptation, into a snare, into many senseless and hurtful desires that plunge men into ruin and destruction. For the love of money is the root of all evils. (1 Timothy 6:7 ff.)

What could be more clear than the fact that our desire to be rich and our construction of an economy built to maximize that desire are plunging us into ruin and destruction? But should not Christians listen to another message —a message emphasizing lack of anxiety about food and clothing, managing with few possessions, finding abundant life in loving, Spirit-filled community? The Christian economist Barbara Ward has written:

In the past, historians tell us, there have been profound revulsions against the aggression, pride and rapacity of human systems. The great ethical systems of mankind—in India, in China, in the Middle East, from the benign wisdom of Confucius to the passionate social protest of the Hebrew prophets—all sought to express an underlying moral reality: we live by moderation, by compassion, by justice; we die by aggression, by pride, by rapacity, and greed.

Now in these latter days, the planet itself in its underlying physical reality repeats the witness of the sages and the prophets. Our collective greeds can degrade and destroy our basic sources of life in air and soil and water. Our collective injustice can continue to create an intolerable imbalance between rich and poor. Envy and fear can unleash the nuclear holocaust. At last, in this age of ultimate scientific discovery, *our facts and our morals have come together to tell us how we must live.*[28]

Implications and Goals

• People should "contribute towards the attainment of the common good of the entire human family as well as to that of their own political community."[29]

• The economic system should make it possible for us to live in active harmony with the environment and, as far as is humanly possible, with the other members of the human family.

• Our economic system should not only serve citizens of the United States, but also promote and enhance the dignity and rights of all members of the human family. Progress in the United States should not be based on exploitation or oppression of other peoples or on damage to the ecosystem, on which all life depends.

• Our economy should be harmonious with a goal of a world where everyone has the basics of food, clothing, shelter, rest, education, health care, and necessary services.[30]

• We should look upon the soil, water, plants, and minerals of the planet as precious endowments, subject to extinction or severe disruption, and needing careful stewardship. The earth should be looked upon as something to "tend" instead of something to exploit.

• Major steps should be taken to control world population in the direction of "zero growth," and subsequently toward a reduction in population through lowered birth rates. Just as important, however, is the reduction of consumption on the part of the people of wealthy nations, because their pollution/resource-use ratio is so much higher than those who live in poor nations.

• The economy should make possible and encourage the drastic reallocation of wealth from rich nations to poor ones, "that there may be equality." (2 Corinthians 8:14)

• Our economic relations with other nations should not sustain oppressive dictatorships or super-rich oligarchies. Our international policy should encourage developing countries to control their own economies to benefit their own people.

• A soaring gross national product should not be the measure of success of the economy. As Edward Albee reportedly said, "Growth for the sake of growth is the ideology of the cancer cell." Any economic growth should be judged in terms of its impact on the environment and on the human family.

• Individuals should be encouraged to find ways to cut back on excess consumption, to give up dependence on ecologically harmful products, to live simply and frugally, and to struggle against covetousness, while creating common social institutions that assure the meeting of their basic needs and keep them from destitution. We should strive to develop the enjoyments and dimensions of life that cause no harm to others or to the environment—art and music, appreciation of nature, gardening, recreation and play, education, personal and interpersonal growth, celebration, worship, and spiritual depth.

• Economic systems should be modeled on simplicity, frugality, recycling, and planning. Wealthy nations such as the United States need to "de-develop" those parts of their economies that are wasteful and harmful in ecological and human terms. (One stimulating analysis concludes that, by elimination of such aspects of our economy, the gross national product could be cut by 50 percent or more, while still meeting people's basic needs.[31]) Rather than an international goal of continued economic growth for wealthy nations, with poorer nations striving to catch up and emulate, the goal should be the de-development of the wealthy nations and the ecologically harmonious development of the poor nations to the point where the basic needs of all "spaceship earth" passengers are met equally.

• New technologies should conform to ecological requirements. Older technologies that are ecologically faulty should be rebuilt.

1. Replacing to a large extent private automobiles (high pollution and high resource use) with mass transit, bicycles, and walking.

2. Replacing nonbiodegradable synthetic materials with natural materials wherever possible.

3. Recycling of all reusable metal, glass, and paper products.

4. Using biological pest control instead of synthetic pesticides.

5. Reducing the need for high energy inputs and using energy that minimizes harm to the ecosystem.

• Reliance on the economic mechanisms of self-interest, profit-seeking, and market regulation has contributed to many of our problems in ecology and planetary human relations. Economic activity should be guided, at least in part, by institutions that focus on the overall common good, that is, by a democratic planning system that measures goals and activities in ecological and human, not in conventional economic, terms.

SECTION II: ACTION FOR CHANGE

Because the subjects of ecology and planetary responsibility are so vast and the possibilities for action so numerous, I will mention only a few suggestions, under the assumption that individual study will suggest enough ideas for action.

Study/Research/Education

Given the seriousness of international injustices and the severity of the threat to human survival, church groups should be doing all they can (through financial support, special conferences, and curricula) to help church people understand the nature of the environmental/planetary crisis. Only with such understanding can we begin to envision and realize an ecologically sound, nonexploitative economic system.

Church Supper with a Twist: Invite the members of your church to a supper on the theme, "Third World Aspirations and Our Responsibility." Have seventeen tables, each with the flag of a different country or the name of a geographical area (Asia, Africa, China) on it. (The reason for the seventeen tables is that the United States represents one-seventeenth of the world's population.) When the church members are seated, place some large garbage cans near the chairs of the persons at the American and European tables and serve them a sumptuous banquet. At the Asian table serve all but one person a small bowl of rice each; at the Latin American table, a small bowl of corn. One person at each of those tables (a member of the planning committee) should receive a fairly substantial, well-balanced meal. Pass out cards showing the difference in per capita consumption in the wealthy and the poor countries.

Have a person from the American and European tables walk over to the tables of the poorer nations and give them small plates of food marked "aid" and "investment," but have them remove from the poorer nations' tables twice as much food as they bring.

If questions are raised by persons at the poor tables, have the person at the table who is being well fed give arguments to justify the system of distribution. If he has difficulty handling objections, have him call in "counter-insurgency forces" from the more wealthy nations to help him out.

Such a supper should lay the basis for a good discussion about our relationship with third world countries. Because the supper may potentially arouse strong emotions, be prepared to help people work through whatever feelings they may have as a result of their participation.

Church Conference: Help to organize an interdenominational conference on "Christian Faith and De-Development." Bring in prominent economists, ecologists, environmental scientists, and theologians to debate the issue of working for a simple, frugal, planned economy.

Small Group: Organize a "Reflection-Action" group to study in depth a particular region of the world, such as Brazil. Read as much as possible about the area and about United States political and economic relationships to it. Bring in resource people, such as visitors from the country, teachers from a local university who have specialized in the area, and members of organizations interested in the area. When enough information is brought together, think through action projects that will bring to public attention any injustices in our relationship to the region.

Action

There are a large number of ecology-action organizations throughout the United States, some organized on a local basis and others with national offices, large budgets, and paid staff. These include: The Environmental Defense Fund,* Environmental Action, Friends of the Earth, National Wildlife Federation, Planned Parenthood/World Population, Scientists' Institute for Public Information, Sierra Club, The Wilderness Society, Zero Population Growth.

Groups working on the question of United States impact on third world countries tend to be smaller and less well-staffed, but they are an extremely important source of information and action ideas. These include: the American Committee on Africa, the Committee of Concerned Asian Scholars, and the North American Congress on Latin America. The Third World Reader Service and the New England Free Press are subscription services that reprint important articles on United States/third world relationships.

Many denominations now have departments or specialized groups that deal with United States/third world relationships. The Roman Catholic "Maryknoll Project for Justice and Peace," for example, publishes a "Third World

---

* See Appendix for addresses.

Packet" with a bibliography of books, films, periodicals, and learning activities for classrooms and discussion groups.

Some very significant church projects have been aimed at using the power of church investments to achieve changes in corporate practices overseas. Denominational groups holding stock in the Gulf Oil Company, for example, have recently issued studies of Gulf's support for colonialism in Angola (a Portuguese colony in Africa) and have sent representatives to Gulf stockholders' meetings to urge changes in the company's policies.

It is unnecessary to list here all the political and organizational action projects that can be undertaken by concerned Christians. My main concern is that, as we engage in action, we ask ourselves: Will the problems be solved by passing some new laws, or do we need to work for whole new sets of values and institutions less likely to produce exploitation and ecological destruction?

Building Alternatives

John Woolman, an eighteenth century Quaker, asked the people of his time to examine "whether the seeds of war have any nourishment in these our possessions."[32] Today, knowing that the 6 percent of the world's population living in the United States lives on 40 percent of the world's annual consumption, we need to ask again whether the seeds of third world exploitation and environmental destruction "reside in these our possessions."

Can we begin to live a new way of life that is less dependent on high consumption of material goods? Is it possible to begin to build an economy without the need for enormous consumption or for exploitation of other nations for their resources—an economy that can operate more harmoniously with the ecosystem? And can such a way of life be a freeing, enabling experience for those who adopt it?

Evidence is accumulating that such a way of life is not only possible, but is beginning to find expression in many parts of the United States. Both Christians and people who do not think of themselves as religious are finding that Jesus' insights about not grasping for money and living a simple life make sense in today's world.

I talked some time ago to a businessman who assured me that it was impossible for him and his family to live decently on less than $15,000 per year. "When you add up the costs of food, housing, clothes, transportation, education, insurance, medical care and all the other expenses," he said, "you just have to work at a job that will earn $15,000 or more."

Only a few years ago, I was in a similar position. As executive director of a social service agency, I was earning $12,000 per year and was spending most of it to support a family of four. Most of my work was with suburban people who had relatively high incomes, but who felt pressure to earn even more to pay off the mortgage and to maintain a middle-class life-style. Husbands felt frustrated by the demands of 9 to 5 jobs, but often worked even longer, which meant more time away from their family. Wives maintained lovely homes, but experienced loneliness, isolation, boredom, and frustration at being too much tied to child care and household tasks with little chance to express fully their personality and creativity.

Two years ago our family moved to the "Philadelphia Life Center," a multigenerational community of about eighty people living in a dozen houses and supporting a nonviolent training center. Each house has several families and/or individuals living together in an "expanded family."

We have chosen to earn an income of less than one-half of our former earnings. Our expenses are now under $5,000 per year for a family of four. We no longer need to hire babysitters because community members share responsibility for children. Using a community garden and a food cooperative, we have cut our food expenses to $25.00 per adult per month. Splitting up house costs among ten people means having to pay only $70 per family per month for housing; community people do house repairs minimally or for no cost. A free medical clinic takes care of most medical problems, and we are working on a mutual aid fund and group insurance to cover emergencies and large medical expenses. Much of our clothing and furniture is handmade or comes from inexpensive shops. We ride bikes, hitchhike, or walk whenever possible to save on transportation costs. Our children attend the local public school, where strong parent action has created a stimulating "open classroom" curriculum.

We are under no illusion that living a simple life-style, in and of itself, will humanize the American economy, and we realize that our way of life is still very comfortable when compared to the conditions under which most people of the world have to live. But we believe that it is important to try to begin to live in a way that, if widely adopted, would help reduce the negative impact of the economy on the ecosystem and on the poorer nations.

Just as important is our discovery that our simple, cooperative way of life frees us in ways that were impossible for us in the past. Men and women are freed to share equally in household tasks, so that no one is unduly burdened with cooking, child care, or cleaning. Both women and men pursue a variety of educational, vocational, and social change interests outside the home. No longer are we tied to the tyranny of nine-to-five jobs, taken only because of the income they produce. Most of us find that we can survive very well on part-time jobs. This gives us the freedom to spend more time working on our interests and on things we believe in and enjoy. We have time to study deeply, to give care to interpersonal relationships, to develop inwardly through prayer and meditation, and to act outwardly by developing nonviolent direct action campaigns. We find all kinds of ways to enjoy one another and the world, whether through songfests, shared work, study groups, common worship, or recreation.

The Life Center is, of course, only one example of this kind of life. It is exciting to observe around the country the growth of Christian and other forms of intentional communities,* beginning to live according to their own values and seeking to work for a new and better society.

---

* For descriptions see W. Paul Jones, "Communes and Christian Intentional Community," *Christian Century,* 90 (January 17, 1973):73; and John Swanson, "Of the Common Life," *Motive,* 31 (February 1971):62.

Nonviolent Direct Action

When I think of direct action, I remember the Pakistani ships and their deadly cargoes; the grateful faces of Bengali seamen whom we took into our homes after they jumped ship, fearful for their lives at the hands of Pakistani sailors; the solemn worship service in front of the White House, with clergy and Bangladesh statesmen reading from the Koran, the Bhagavad Gita, and the Bible, and a communion meal with rice replacing bread and wine; the fellowship of marches and fasts and vigils as we strove to bring to public attention the horror of the massacre 10,000 miles away and our involvement, as United States taxpayers, in it. Such extraordinary activities sometimes fail, but this one worked, which suggests again that people working together (even a very few) are able to make a big difference.

Many of my deepest experiences in life, the times when I have felt closest to God and to other human beings, have come when I have acted with others to challenge injustice and oppression, while striving to love and understand those fellow human beings who perpetuate oppression. My feeling is that we will be called upon more and more to engage in strong but loving action as we seek to be open to the shalom that God intends for humanity.

Questions for Discussion

1. Are the present trade, aid, and investment practices of the wealthy nations capable of building a world economic community based on justice?
2. How serious is the ecological crisis we face? Can technology save us from resource-depletion and over-pollution?
3. Is continued economic growth desirable?
4. Is our affluence based on unjust exploitation of other nations? In what way?
5. Is it realistic to work for the "de-development" of the United States? Is such a goal desirable?

6. What kind of economic system would do the most to create harmony with the environment and with the rest of the world family?

Suggested Readings

Barnet, Richard J. *Intervention and Revolution*. New York: World, 1968. In-depth study of many United States interventions to counter movements for social change in other nations.

"A Blueprint for Survival," *The Ecologist* 2 (January, 1972). Distinguished British scientists describe the environmental crisis and offer far-reaching solutions.

Camara, Helder. *Church and Colonialism*. Denville, N.J.: Dimension Books, 1969. A Brazilian Catholic Bishop speaks out against the exploitation of poor nations by rich ones.

Commoner, Barry. *The Closing Circle*. New York: Knopf, 1971. Packed with information on ecology and economics.

Ehrlich, Paul R. and Ehrlich, Anne H. *Population, Resources and Environment: Issues in Human Ecology*. San Francisco: W. H. Freeman, 1972. A comprehensive resource book on ecology.

Ehrlich, Paul R., and Harriman, Richard L. *How to Be a Survivor*. New York: Ballantine, 1971. The requisites of survival in light of ecological realities.

Johnson, Warren A., and Hardesty, John. *Economic Growth vs. the Environment*. Belmont, Calif.: Wadsworth, 1971. Economic growth is questioned as unnecessary and destructive to the environment.

Magdoff, Harry. *The Age of Imperialism: The Economics of U.S. Foreign Policy*. New York: Monthly Review Press, 1969. The demands of our economy often cast us in the role of exploiter overseas.

Meadows, Donella H., et al. *The Limits to Growth*. New York: Signet Books, 1972. A controversial book using computer models to argue for an end to economic growth and the adoption of a steady-state economy.

Conclusion

The God portrayed in the Bible is at work in the world, calling humans to cooperate with him in correcting injustice, overcoming oppression, and building societies where his children can live together in shalom. The struggle for economic justice is a crucial aspect of this work.

There are some features of our economy about which we can be proud, but there are other features that point to a chasm between biblical values and our economic practices. Too often we neglect the needy and turn aside the way of the afflicted. Our institutions create vast inequalities between the very rich and the very poor, between the very powerful and those who have little control over their lives. Our precious heritage of political democracy is undercut by the corrupting influence of great wealth. We are urged to strive for private profit and individual aggrandizement rather than for the common good. Our drive to consume and to grow exploits the earth, damages the ecosystem, and too often hurts the people of poorer nations.

As Christians we are called to struggle for a greater embodiment of economic justice in our nation. As we study the "good things" that are part of our own heritage, and as we see how other nations have moved ahead, we begin to develop a feeling for how economic life in our own country could be more just, cooperative, and loving. We begin to sense how we can work together for a society more in harmony with God's shalom.

There are those who may think that it is inappropriate to try to encompass "religion" and "economics" in the same book. Henry Cadbury, Emeritus Professor of Divinity at Harvard Divinity School, worked with the group of scholars who brought out the Revised Standard Version of the Bible. He was also for many years chairman of the social-activist American Friends Service Committee. A story is told about a reporter who asked Cadbury how he could combine two such contradictory themes in one life.

The reporter pointed out that on the one hand Cadbury was doing the most abstruse kind of biblical scholarship, poring over ancient texts in Greek and Hebrew. On the other hand, through the American Friends Service Committee, he was involved in all kinds of worldly activities, like the peace movement, relief to hungry people, prison reform, international reconciliation.

"How do you explain such an apparent contradiction?" the reporter asked.

Henry Cadbury thought for a moment, then answered: "They both involve translating the Bible."

That is what we have tried to do in this book.

Appendix

Footnotes

Introduction
1. *Faith and Practice of the Philadelphia Yearly Meeting of the Religious Society of Friends: A Book of Christian Discipline* (1515 Cherry St., Philadelphia, 1955), p. 233.
2. Queries of the Two Philadelphia Yearly Meetings of Friends (Philadelphia, 1949), leaflet.
3. I spent one summer in Scandinavia, studying in particular Sweden's prison system, new towns, medical care, cooperatives, and efforts to eliminate poverty.

I. A Theology of Economic Justice
1. Smith's reference to the "invisible hand" is found in his monumental *The Wealth of Nations* (New York: Modern Library, 1937), p. 423. A modern economist says of Smith: "What he sought was 'the invisible hand,' as he called it, whereby 'the private interests and passions of man' are led in the direction 'which is most agreeable to the interests of the whole society.'" Robert Heilbroner, *The Worldly Philosophers* (New York: Simon and Schuster, 1967), p. 49.
2. Heilbroner, *The Worldly Philosophers,* says that the thought of the great economists, of which Smith was one, "shaped and swayed the world" (p. 11) and that the impact of their opinions "constitute nothing less than the gradual construction of the architecture of contemporary life" (p. 13). "After Smith had displayed the first true tableau of modern society," he writes, "all of the Western World became the world of Adam Smith" (p. 37).
3. Milton Friedman, "The Social Responsibility of Business Is to Increase Its Profits," *The New York Times Magazine* (September 13, 1970): 32.
4. Richard Lichtman, *Toward Community* (Santa Barbara, Calif.: Center for the Study of Democratic Institutions, 1966), p. 10.
5. Abraham J. Heschel, *The Prophets* (New York: Harper and Row, 1962), p. 3. Used by permission.
6. *Ibid.,* p. 4.
7. *Ibid.,* p. 32.
8. *Ibid.,* p. 216.
9. *Ibid.,* p. 167.
10. Rabbi Abraham J. Heschel, "The Religious Basis of Equality of Opportunity," speech at the National Conference on Religion and Race, Chicago, January 14–17, 1963.
11. Quoted in David Kirk, *Quotations from Chairman Jesus* (New York: Bantam Books, 1969), p. 144. Used by permission of Templegate Publications.
12. Henry David Thoreau, *Walden* (New York: Rinehart, 1948), p. 67.
13. William N. Loucks and William G. Whitney, *Comparative Economic Systems* (New York: Harper and Row, 1969), p. 20.

14. Charles M. Laymon, ed., *The Interpreter's One-Volume Commentary on the Bible* (Nashville, Tenn.: Abingdon, 1971), p. 83.
15. See the 1954 statement of the General Board of the National Council of Churches, "Christian Principles and Assumptions for Economic Life," in *The Christian Century 71* (October 13, 1954): 1234. "God is the only absolute owner. Every Christian particularly should look upon all of his [sic] possessions, as well as his talents, as a trustee, and should use them in the light of his understanding of God's purposes for him."
16. Nels F. S. Ferré, *Christianity and Society* (New York: Harper and Row, 1950), pp. 224–225. Used by permission.
17. Robert C. Dentan, "The Kingdom of God in the Old Testament," in *The Interpreter's One-Volume Commentary*, p. 1159.
18. *Ibid.*, p. 1165.
19. National Council of Churches, *op. cit.*, p. 1234.
20. See Edward A. Powers, *Signs of Shalom* (Philadelphia: United Church Press, 1973), pp. 9–10.
21. Ralph Weltge, "Shalom is. . . ," *Colloquy* 5 (July–August, 1972): 2. Used by permission.
22. Walter Brueggemann, "Living Toward a Vision," *Colloquy* 5 (July–August, 1972): 7. Used by permission.
23. Gabriel Fackre, "Realism and Vision," *Christianity and Crisis* 30 (April 13, 1970): 74.
24. Quoted in Joseph R. Barndt, "Christianity and Marxism in Chile," *The Christian Century* 89 (June 7, 1972): 653.
25. "Love calls us to form an ideal of the kind of economic community that would best provide for the persons and total world community which the spirit of Christ leads us to envisage. Then with all possible technical aid we must support policies best calculated to lead toward realization of these ideals." L. Harold DeWolf, *Responsible Freedom* (New York: Harper and Row, 1971), p. 272.

II. The Economic Structures of the United States

1. "Senate Unit Told of Hunger in U.S.," *The New York Times*, 23 January 1969, p. 1. See also mimeographed "Statement by Arnold E. Schaeffer, Chief, Nutrition Program, Division of Chronic Disease Programs, Regional Medical Programs Service, Health Services and Mental Health Administration, Department of Health, Education and Welfare, before Senate Select Committee on Nutrition and Related Human Needs, January 22, 1969.
2. Citizens' Board of Inquiry into Hunger and Malnutrition in the United States, *Hunger, U.S.A.* (Washington, D.C.: New Community Press, 1968), p. 9.
3. Nick Kotz, *Let Them Eat Promises* (Englewood Cliffs, N.J.: Prentice-Hall, 1969), pp. 136–137.
4. "Hollings Fight on Hunger Is Stirring the South," *The New York Times*, 8 March 1969, p. 14. Also see Kotz, *Promises*, pp. 196 ff.
5. "Farewell to Poverty, Hail to Hunger," Art Buchwald, *Philadelphia Sunday Bulletin*, 23 March, 1969.
6. Kotz, *Promises*, Foreword, p. ix.
7. *Ibid.*, p. 194.
8. *Hunger, U.S.A. Revisited, A Report of the Citizens' Board of*

Inquiry into Hunger and Malnutrition in the United States (Washington, D.C.: National Council on Hunger and Malnutrition and the Southern Regional Council, October, 1972), p. 5.

9. Robert L. Heilbroner, *The Economic Problem* (Englewood Cliffs, N.J.: Prentice-Hall, 1968), p. 8.

10. "An interview with Jesse Jackson," *Playboy* (November, 1969).

11. "Median Income $10,285, But Inflation Cancels Gain," *The New York Times,* 18 July 1972, p. 1.

12. "Worker Benefits Held Inadequate in National Study," *The New York Times*, 31 July 1972, p. 1.

13. Report of the President's Commission on Income Maintenance Programs, *Poverty Amid Plenty* (Washington, D.C.: U.S. Government Printing Office, 1969), p. 2.

14. Robert S. Diamond, "A Self-Portrait of the Chief Executive," *Fortune* 81 (May, 1970): 181.

15. *Economic Report of the President, 1969* (Washington, D.C.: U.S. Government Printing Office, 1969), p. 175.

16. National Commission on Urban Problems, *Building the American City* (Washington, D.C.: U.S. Government Printing Office, 1968), p. 67. According to a study by the U.S. Government Accounting Office, urban renewal has torn down 3.5 housing units for every one it put up, with most of the housing destroyed being that of poor and middle-income people.

17. "Doctors' Median Income ($40,550) Spurs Fierce Debate," *The New York Times*, 13 September 1971, p. 29.

18. Robert L. Heilbroner, "Benign Neglect in the United States," *Transaction* 7 (October, 1970): 16.

19. Ralph Nader, "The Great Pension Fraud," *The Progressive* 35 (October, 1971): 18–20.

20. "Chemical Debris Fouling Vast Areas of Atlantic," *The New York Times*, 13 February 1973, p. 1.

21. Speech before the American Bar Association, Dallas, Texas, October, 1969.

22. Richard G. Watts in *Presbyterian Life* 17 (June 1, 1964): 37–39. Copyright *Presbyterian Life.* Used by permission.

III. Justice and Human Need

1. *Philadelphia Inquirer*, 18 December 1972, p. 1.

2. Office of Economic Opportunity, *The Poor in 1970: A Chartbook,* quoted in *Hunger, U.S.A. Revisited,* Appendix I.

3. *A "Freedom Budget" for All Americans* (New York: A. Philip Randolph Institute, 1966), p. 27.

4. Report of the President's Commission on Income Maintenance Programs, *Poverty Amid Plenty,* p. 2. Among the distinguished members of the Commission were Ben W. Heineman, Chairman, Northwest Industries, Inc.; James W. Aston, Chairman of the Board, Republic National Bank of Dallas; D. C. Burnham, Chairman, Westinghouse Electric Co.; and Thomas J. Watson, Board Chairman, IBM Corporation.

5. See "Worker Benefits Held Inadequate in National Study," *The New York Times,* 31 July 1972, p. 1.

6. See Ralph Nader, "The Great Pension Fraud," p. 18.

7. "Senate Panel Says Federal Programs Fail to Meet Needs of Elderly," *The New York Times*, 15 April 1971, p. 24.

8. "3.1 Million Elderly Still Below Poverty Line," *Philadelphia Inquirer*, 15 January 1973, p. 2-A.

9. *Ibid.*

10. Michael Harrington, "Housing Units Lost in Renewal Program," *Philadelphia Evening Bulletin*, 1 November 1970, section 1-J, p. 26.

11. Edward Kennedy, "National Health Insurance and Health Security," *Congressional Record*, 27 August 1970, p. 30142.

12. See David M. Cleary, *Europe's Differing Health Plans* (Philadelphia: *Evening Bulletin* reprint, 1970), which shows that *many* European countries spend proportionately less on health care than the United States while getting better services.

13. *Statistical Yearbook* (New York: United Nations, 1966), pp. 108–110.

14. *Programme of the Swedish Social Democratic Labor Party* (Stockholm, 1960), p. 14.

15. Donald S. Connery, *The Scandinavians* (New York: Simon and Schuster, 1966), p. 244, emphasis added.

16. Jack A. Underhill, "European New Towns: One Answer to Urban Problems?" *HUD Challenge* (published by the U.S. Department of Housing and Urban Development) 1 (March–April, 1970): 19.

17. Sig Gissler, "Cities for Living: Europe Plans Ahead," *The Progressive* 35 (November, 1971):42. Used by permission.

18. Martin Luther King, Jr., *Why We Can't Wait* (New York: Signet Books, 1964), p. 137.

19. *A "Freedom Budget" for All Americans.*

20. Milton Friedman, *Capitalism and Freedom* (Chicago: University of Chicago Press, 1965), pp. 192 ff.; Robert Theobald, ed., *The Guaranteed Income* (New York: Doubleday and Company, 1966). pp. 15 ff.

21. Report of the National Commission on Technology, Automation and Economic Progress, *Technology and the American Economy* (Washington, D.C.: U.S. Government Printing Office, 1966). The Commission estimated (see p. 36) that *5.3 million* useful jobs could be created through public service employment in such areas as parks, streets, schools, slum areas, libraries, hospitals, etc.

22. *Ibid.*, p. 36.

23. "Income Aid Plan Based on Need Proposed by Presidential Panel," *The New York Times*, 13 November 1969, p. 1.

24. See, for example, "Recommendations for National Action" in *Report of the National Advisory Commission on Civil Disorders* (New York: Bantam Books, 1968), pp. 410 ff.

25. Ron W. Jones, Julia Cheever, and Ferry Ficklin, *Finding Community* (Palo Alto, Calif.: James E. Freel and Associates, 1971), pp. 48–50.

26. Arthur and Stuart Frank, *The People's Handbook of Medical Care* (New York: Vintage, 1972).

IV. Inequality: Super-Rich and Super-Poor

1. "Mrs. Horace Dodge Dies at 103; Among World's Richest Women," *The New York Times*, 4 June 1970, p. 43.

2. *Ibid.*

3. *Ibid.*

4. "Billionaire Texan Fights Social Ills," *The New York Times,* 28 November 1969, p. 41.

5. "Nijinsky's Last Dance," *Newsweek* 76 (October 18, 1970): 73.

6. "Officers Salaries Rise at Big Banks," *The New York Times,* 16 March 1970, p. 65.

7. "Top Executives Got Raises Averaging 14% in 1971," *Philadelphia Inquirer,* 20 April 1972, p. 1.

8. See Ferdinand Lundberg, *The Rich and the Super-Rich* (New York: Lyle Stuart, 1968). The following statement about business perquisites is found in Gabriel Kolko's *Wealth and Power in America* (New York: Frederick A. Praeger, 1962), p. 19. "In 1954 37% of the Cadillacs registered in Manhattan and 20% of those registered in Philadelphia were in the names of businesses. Some 80% of the check totals of the most expensive restaurants and 30 to 40% of Broadway theater tickets are covered by expense accounts. Most of the items charged to Diners' Club, American Express, and other luxury credit cards by members, who numbered well over a million, are paid for by businesses. One-half of the executives in small companies and one-third of those in large companies are reimbursed for their expenses in social clubs and organizations. More than one-half of the executives in small firms and more than one-quarter of those in large companies are provided with private automobiles. One-fifth of the large corporations have their own country clubs and resorts for their executives. . . . One corporation president spent $17,000 of company funds on an African safari; another charged to business expenses $65,000 in jewelry, $22,000 in liquor, $35,000 in nightclub tabs, $25,000 in gifts, and $16,000 in boat outlays." (From *Wealth and Power in America:* An Analysis of Social Class and Income Distribution, by Gabriel Kolko. © 1962 by Frederick A. Praeger, Inc., New York. Excerpted and reprinted by permission.)

9. *Louis Kelso—The Second Income Plan,* notes from a slide show, mimeographed.

10. Robert Heilbroner, *The Limits of American Capitalism* (New York: Harper and Row, 1965), pp. 11–12.

11. Letitia Upton and Nancy Lyons, *Basic Facts: Distribution of Personal Income and Wealth in the United States* (Cambridge: Cambridge Institute booklet, May, 1972), pp. 1–2. Used by permission.

12. *Ibid.,* p. 1.

13. *Ibid.,* p. 6, emphasis added.

14. From a report by Chairman Wright Patman of the House Banking Committee, U.S. House of Representatives, reported in Tristran Coffin's newsletter, *Washington Watch* 22 (September 1, 1972):3. See also the speech by Abram T. Collier, President of the New England Mutual Life Insurance Co., "The Relevance of Capital" (pamphlet, May, 1968), in which he claims that "slightly more than 2% of the households of this country own 80% of the nation's productive capital, while 5 to 8% own most of the rest." See also Upton and Lyons, *Basic Facts,* p. 9.

15. Upton and Lyons, *Basic Facts,* p. 3.

16. *Ibid.,* p. 4.

17. "Operation Open Up the System," *Report from Washington* 2 (October 10, 1972): 16.

18. *Ibid.*, p. 16.
19. *Ibid.*, p. 17.
20. *Ibid.*, p. 17.
21. Mark J. Green, James M. Fallows, and David R. Zwick, *Who Runs Congress?* (New York: Bantam Books, 1972), pp. 7–8.
22. U.S. Department of Health, Education and Welfare, "Estimated Employability of Recipients of Public Assistance Money Payments" (Washington, D.C.: U.S. Government Printing Office, July, 1968).
23. Staff Study, Joint Economic Committee, Congress of the United States, *The Economics of Federal Subsidy Programs* (Washington, D.C.: U.S. Government Printing Office, January 11, 1971).
24. Taylor Branch, "Government Subsidies: Who Gets the $63 Billion?" *Washington Monthly* 4 (March, 1972): 12. Used by permission.
25. "China Visit Shows Change of 25 Years," *The New York Times,* 19 April 1971, p. 10.
26. *Experiment Without Precedent* (Philadelphia: American Friends Service Committee, 1972), p. 14. Used by permission.
27. Louis Kraar, "I Have Seen China—and They Work," *Fortune* 86 (August, 1972):112.
28. Alexander Casella, "Mao's China, 1972: A Nostalgia for Yenan, 1935," *The New York Times Magazine* (February 20, 1972): 30.
29. Naphtali Golomb, "Managing Without Sanctions or Rewards," *Management of Personnel Quarterly* (Summer 1968):24.
30. U.S. Department of Health, Education and Welfare, *Work in America* (Washington, D.C.: U.S. Government Printing Office, 1972).
31. Stewart Alsop, "The American Class System," *Newsweek* 75 (June 29, 1970):88. Copyright *Newsweek*, Inc. 1970, reprinted by permission.
32. "Tax Reform Issue Boosts McGovern," *Philadelphia Inquirer,* 9 October 1972, p. 5.
33. See Louis O. Kelso and Patricia Hetter, *Two-Factor Theory: The Economics of Reality* (New York: Vintage, 1968); and Louis O. Kelso and Mortimer J. Adler, *The Capitalist Manifesto* (New York: Random House, 1958).
34. *Business and Society Review* 1 (Spring, 1972):54.
35. Robert A. Dahl, *After the Revolution?* (New Haven: Yale University Press, 1970), pp. 115–139.
36. See Nels F. S. Ferré, *Christianity and Society*, p. 230: "Obviously, there must be no reward except for labor, no reward for speculative activity or 'finagling' of finances, no living on the work of others without personal contribution to it, except, of course, for those unable to work, who have all the rights and privileges of those who can."
37. *Ibid.*, p. 229.
38. Ron W. Jones, et al., op cit., pp. 14–15.

V. A Family Riding on Spaceship Earth

1. "Pakistan: All in the Family," *Newsweek* 79 (January 10, 1972): 26.
2. Information from the *Defense Monitor,* 1 (September 8, 1972): 1,5. A publication of the Center for Defense Information, an inde-

pendent, non-governmental organization staffed (at the time of this issue) by a retired Navy Rear Admiral and a retired Air Force Lieutenant Colonel.

3. Michael T. Klare, "America's Global Police," *American Report* (September 15, 1972): 2.

4. James Armstrong, " 'The People Are Doing . . . Badly' in Brazil," *The Christian Century* 88 (January 6, 1971):14.

5. William Wipfler, "The Price of 'Progress' in Brazil," *Christianity and Crisis* (March 16, 1970): 44.

6. "Latin American Economies Take Mixed Course," *The New York Times,* 10 July 1972, p. 45.

7. Armstrong, *The People,* p. 14–16.

8. "Latin American Economies Take Mixed Course," *The New York Times.*

9. Dwight D. Eisenhower, *Mandate for Change: Vol. I: The White House Years, 1953–1956* (New York: Doubleday and Co., 1963), pp. 420–427. See also Richard J. Barnet, *Intervention and Revolution* (New York: World Publishing Company, 1968), pp. 229–236.

10. Gunnar Myrdal, *The Challenge of World Poverty* (New York: Pantheon Books, 1970), p. 456. Used by permission.

11. Barnet, *Intervention and Revolution.*

12. Everett Dirksen, "National Commitments," *Congressional Record* (June 23, 1969): 16840–16843.

13. "Transcript of President Nixon's Conference on Foreign and Domestic Matters," *The New York Times*, 17 September 1971, p. 27.

14. David S. French, "Does the U.S. Exploit the Developing Nations?" *Commonweal* 86 (May 19, 1967): 257–259.

15. Dom Helder Camara, *The Church and Colonialism* (Denville, N.J.: Dimension Books, 1969), p. 106.

16. U.S. Department of Commerce, *Survey of Current Business* (October, 1971):35.

17. Myrdal, *World Poverty,* p. 322. Used by permission.

18. "Farewell to Foreign Aid: A Liberal Takes Leave," *Congressional Record* (October 29, 1971): 38257.

19. Myrdal, *World Poverty,* p. 455. Used by permission.

20. *Ibid.,* pp. 263–265.

21. "The Masked Men," *Newsweek* 81 (January 22, 1973): 44.

22. Robert Heilbroner, "Ecological Armageddon," in Warren A. Johnson and John Hardesty, *Economic Growth vs. the Environment* (Belmont, Calif.: Wadsworth, 1971), p. 39.

23. "The Worst Is Yet to Be?" *Time* 99 (January 24, 1972): 37.

24. An estimate by Sir Peter Medwar, whom *The New York Times* (December 14, 1970) called "one of the great scientific figures of the Western World."

25. Paul Ehrlich, "The Population Bomb," *The New York Times,* 4 November 1970, p. 47.

26. Barry Commoner, *The Closing Circle* (New York: Knopf, 1971), pp. 250 ff.

27. Quoted in *The Christian Century* 89 (November 29, 1972): 1210.

28. Barbara Ward, "Only One Earth," lecture at Stockholm, June, 1972, emphasis added. Used by permission of the International Institute for Environmental Affairs. The Stockholm lectures are

available in both hard and soft cover under the title, "Who Speaks for Earth?" (published by W. W. Norton, New York).

29. Pope John XXIII, *Pacem in Terris.*

30. *Universal Declaration of Human Rights,* Adopted by the United Nations, November 10, 1948.

31. John Hardesty, et al., "The Political Economy of Environmental Destruction," in *Economic Growth vs. the Environment,* op. cit., p. 95.

32. *John Woolman Speaks* (Brooklyn, New York: Leonard S. Kenworthy, 1945), p. 5.

Addresses

Below are the addresses of groups mentioned in the text. Many of them have local chapters as well as national offices.

Justice and Human Need

United Farm Workers Organizing Committee, P.O. Box 130, Delano, California 93215

National Welfare Rights Organization, 1419 H Street, N.W., Washington, D.C. 20005

National Tenants' Organization, 425 13th St., N.W., Washington, D.C. 20004

Southern Conference Educational Fund, 3210 W. Broadway, Louisville, Kentucky 40211

League for Industrial Democracy, 112 E. 19th Street, New York, New York 10003

Southern Christian Leadership Conference, 322 Auburn Avenue, N.E., Atlanta, Georgia 30303

Institute for Policy Studies, 1520 New Hampshire Avenue, N.W., Washington, D.C. 20006

New Priorities Movement, 490 Riverside Drive, New York, New York 10027

Movement for a New Society, 4722 Baltimore Avenue, Philadelphia, Pennsylvania 19143

Medical Committee for Human Rights, 710 S. Marshfield, Chicago, Illinois 60612

People's Architecture, 2326 Sacramento, Berkeley, California 94702

Psychologists for Social Action, Box 463, Planetarium Station, New York, New York 10024

Computer People for Peace, 291 Sterling Place, Brooklyn, New York 11238

Scientists and Engineers for Social and Political Action, 9 Walden Street, Jamaica Plain, Massachusetts 02130

Society for Social Responsibility in Science, 221 Rock Hill Road, Bala Cynwyd, Pennsylvania 19004

Union of Radical Political Economists, 2503 Student Activities Building, The University of Michigan, Ann Arbor, Michigan 48104

People's Fund, 1307 Sansom Street, Philadelphia, Pennsylvania 19107

Macro-Analysis Collective, 4719 Cedar Avenue, Philadelphia, Pennsylvania 19143

Inequality: Super-Rich and Super-Poor

Common Cause, 2030 M St., N.W., Washington, D.C. 20036

Exploratory Project for Economic Alternatives, 5 Arlington Street, Cambridge, Massachusetts 02140

New Town Project, 95 Fayerweather Street, Cambridge, Massachusetts 02138

New Communities, Inc.: write International Independence Institute, West Road, Box 183, Ashby, Massachusetts 01431

The Cooperative League of the U.S.A., 1828 L Street, N.W., Washington, D.C. 20036

A Family Riding on Spaceship Earth

Environmental Defense Fund, P.O. Drawer 740, Stony Brook, New York 11790

Environmental Action, 1346 Connecticut Avenue, N.W., Room 731, Washington, D.C. 20036

Friends of the Earth, 30 E. 42nd Street, New York, New York 10017

The National Wildlife Federation, 1412 16th St., N.W., Washington, D.C. 20036

Planned Parenthood/World Population, 515 Madison Avenue, New York, New York 10022

Scientists' Institute for Public Information, 30 E. 68th Street, New York, New York 10021

The Sierra Club, 1050 Mills Tower, San Francisco, California 94104

The Wilderness Society, 729 15th Street, N.W., Washington, D.C. 20005

Zero Population Growth, 367 State Street, Los Altos, California 94022

The American Committee on Africa, 164 Madison Avenue, New York, New York 10016

The Committee of Concerned Asian Scholars, 9 Sutter Street, San Francisco, California 94104

North American Congress on Latin America, Box 57, Cathedral Park Station, New York, New York 10025

Maryknoll Project for Justice and Peace, 110 Walsh Building, Maryknoll, New York 10545

Third World Reader Service, 1500 Farragut Street, N.W., Washington, D.C. 20011

New England Free Press, 791 Tremont Street, Room 401, Boston, Massachusetts 02118

Philadelphia Life Center, 1006 S. 46th Street, Philadelphia, Pennsylvania 19143

31